OLD AS DIRT
— SO WHAT!

by

LES BLAIR

Cover Design and Illustrations by John Pyle

ABOUT THE AUTHOR

Les Blair is convinced that one needs to be equipped with three things to face the aging clock and its problems,--a healthy spirituality, a positive attitude and a quick sense of humor. He has approached old age with a wonderful "tongue in cheek" humor in the first parts of this book, but also seriously looks at a better way to approach the inevitable aging process. All this is a result from his considerable research and observation on the subject and by drawing on personal experiences from his own life.

Since 1966 when Les published his first cookbook he has continued his interest in writing. This is his eleventh book. Ozark cooking, humor and customs have been a favorite theme in previous books and he has approached the subject of old age in the same spirit.

For many years, Les and wife Geanie have made a living making candies to be sold at Ozark-Maid Candies. Their son Alan is now the owner of this business.

Along with writing, his hobbies include leaded glass art, wood carving, painting — and fishing. He is a long time resident of Osage Beach, Missouri, where he continues to enjoy his retirement years.

OLD AS DIRT — SO WHAT!

OLD AS DIRT — SO WHAT!

PREFACE

This is a book on aging. You might ask, "Are you qualified to write such a book?" No, not if you base it on a degree or formal schooling on gerontology, or any formal study on aging. I do not consider myself an "authority"on much of anything, much less aging, but I do feel qualified to write this book, and there was a definite need for it. Let my tell you why by relating a quick bio and some of my beliefs:

I am 74 years old, and have been experiencing and observing the aging process for a number of years. In other words, I have been "researching"and observing the facets and mannerisms of aging for a long time. All those years and experiences, I believe, has led me to a pretty accurate feel for what the aging process is all about.

I started graying in my 30's and now have completely white hair. I did succumb to vanity and colored my hair for a short time, until I realized how foolish I looked. I have experienced minor medical problems over the years. I now have Osteoarthritis (related to the age process), and Rheumatoid Arthritis (not age-related.) The medical problems are not pleasant, but early-on I became a believer in that old saying, "I used to bemoan having no shoes — until I met a man who had no feet." It is true that you can always find someone who has more problems than you.

Incidentally, I am a Christian, and feel I have a healthy spirituality. I am thankful to God to be as healthy physically as I am. Also, I am by nature an optimist, and I truly am thankful for that. Since my 30's, I have developed a simple philosophy and attitude about growing old. I feel that each stage of my life has been good, better than the one before. The terms "young," "middle-aged" or "old" mean nothing to me, except to classify the stage of life I was or am now in. I have never had the desire to go back to a former stage of my life.

You hear people express the desire: "Oh, if I were only young again." You will never hear that from me. I am "old as dirt" now and honestly do not want to go back to being young. It would be nice to have fewer health problems and more energy, but I feel I would lose too much to go back, if it were possible. I lay no claim to being wise or brilliant, but have gained a lot of knowledge through experience, observation and study, and I would not trade that for youth. Also, I am more settled and serene, which is valuable to enjoying living.

I am a firm believer that you must face the inevitability of growing old with the right thankfulness, positive attitude and cheerful outlook. It can make the difference between enjoyment of your life and misery. There is no doubt that growing old is mandatory, and also no doubt that growing up is optional. In other words, we have no choice about aging, but we certainly can chose how we face and spend our later years. There is absolutely nothing you can do to stop the aging process, so you must choose one of two methods to approach it.

The wrong method is to approach it with dread, dwell on the negative aspects, such as poorer health, lessened abilities, and self-pity — eventually leading to a state of bitterness and absolute misery. I firmly believe that life is so short and precious that the only correct way to approach old age is with a positive attitude — the only way to have a fruitful and happy time in those years you have left to live. Then, when it comes to your death, you will have no regrets for the way you lived.

I believe we not only have a chronological age, measured in years, we also have a psychological age — determined by the way we feel, act and react to people and circumstances. Looking at your life with a positive attitude and good humor will actually make you feel and even look younger. Humor and laughter are good for our well-being, and help us keep our balance when we meet life's events, and help us communicate with those who are younger.

Laughter at oneself in awkward situations is important to remove any embarrassment. It is also very therapeutic. There is truth in the old adage, "You don't stop laughing because you are old, but you are old if you stop laughing." I firmly believe that people who laugh will live longer, and much of their health depends on being able to laugh. The bottom line: I am convinced that one needs to be equipped with three things to face the aging clock and its problems,--a healthy spirituality, a positive attitude and a quick sense of humor.

Friends are important. My wife and I have a circle of good friends with whom we have an enjoyable time. We see each other during worship and Bible study on Sunday, and many times go to lunch together, always enjoying each other's company. During Wednesday evening Bible study we have a good time, having a good deal of laughter along with serious Bible study. We often retire to McDonalds for refreshments and more visiting. We have learned to laugh at ourselves with others in this circle. We really connect and enjoy each others company, and are a support group when any one of us is hurting — physically or mentally. I have friends with whom I have sat on a porch, rocking perhaps, saying only a few words — and going away feeling that I have had great communication.

So far this has been all about me. Now let's talk about this book — divided into three books. It is a multi-faceted book meant to serve some definite purposes: First, to help those who are facing the aging clock to see aspects of humor in their own circumstances and give them a better attitude to face those things. Next, to remove from their minds some commonly held myths about aging and replace them with truths. And finally, to inspire them to approach their own aging process in such a way that it will perhaps be one of the most enjoyable periods of their lives. I sincerely hope it does at least one if not all of these things for you.

The first book, "TIME FLIES WHETHER YOU ARE HAVING FUN OR NOT," is a "tongue in cheek" humorous narrative of many of the elements of the aging process: wrinkles and wattles, hair graying, loss & baldness, lessened arm and leg function, deteriorating muscles, memory loss, vision and hearing loss, lessened sex drive, etc. It is also about some of the amusing traits, actions and mannerisms of those growing old. I over-emphasize in much of my narration, but remember, it is to amuse you and help you see the humor in your own situation.

The second book, "FIELD GUIDE FOR OLD GEEZER / GEEZERETTES," is again another tongue in cheek narrative of some of the amusing (and sometimes aggravating) traits of some older people. Read them, and you will recall witnessing or being a participant in some of these examples. It will make you more aware of them, and perhaps avoid being one with those traits. Again, I exaggerate in much of my description. This is in fun although you will actually see many old people with these actions or mannerisms.

The final book, "AGING: PROBLEMS—MYTHS & TRUTHS—SOLUTIONS," is, as the title implies, first—a frank and serious discussion of several of the problems of aging (real or imagined) one faces. Secondly, an attempt to remove from people's minds many commonly held myths or misconceptions about aging with the truths about those matters. Lastly, solutions to the aforementioned problems are given, meant to inspire aging people to make their latter years some of the most pleasant.

I pray that this book will help its readers face their own aging clock with the right attitude, good humor, and perhaps even a healthy spirituality. If this book changes even one person's attitude toward life and aging — it will have been worth the effort.

May God Bless and give you joy — Les Blair

Age is a quality of the mind:
If you have left your dreams behind,
If hope is cold;
If you no longer look ahead,
If your ambition's fires are dead —
Then you are old.
But if from life you take the best,
And if in life you keep the jest
If love you hold;
No matter how the years go by,
No matter how the birthdays fly—
You are not old.
— Edward Tuck

"Let me but live my life from year to year,
With forward face and unreluctant soul.
Not hurrying to, nor turning from the goal;
Not mourning for things that disappear
In the dim past, nor holding back in fear
From what the future veils, but wit a whole
And happy heart, that pays its toll
To you and age, and travels on with cheer.
So let the way wind up the hill or down,
O'er rough or smooth, the journey will be joy;
Still seeking what I sought when but a boy,
New friendship, high adventure, and a crown,
I shall grow old, but never lose life's zest,
Because the road's last turn will be the best."
— Henry van Dyke

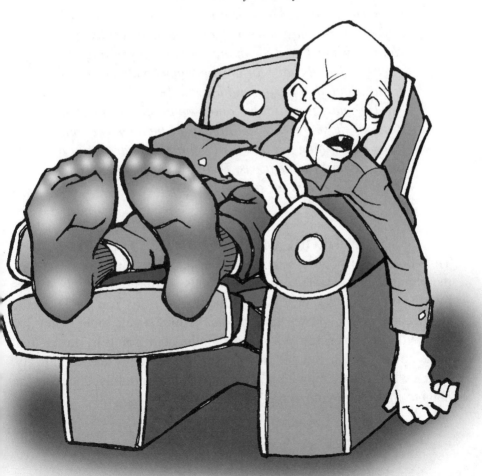

BOOK I

TIME FLIES — WHETHER YOU'RE HAVING FUN OR NOT

*[This is a tongue in cheek narrative of many of the ele-
ments of the aging process: wrinkles & wattles, hair
graying or loss & baldness, lessened dexterity, deteriorating muscles, memory loss, vision and hearing loss,
lessened sex drive, etc. I will be using the mirror anal-
ogy often, because mirrors are related to vanity, and
vanity has much to do with our outlook on growing old.
I believe there is hope for any person who can put aside
vanity, look in a mirror and laugh at what he sees.*

*This narrative is also about some of the amusing
traits of those growing old. Some of the elements and
traits concerning sex and bodily functions carry with it
some rather graphic terms. Please don't be offended —
they are necessary for a complete narrative.]*

THE THEORY OF AGE/TIME RELATIVITY

Time does fly. I believe, just as Darwin had the Theory of Relativity,
there must be an Age/Time Relativity. This is a basic Relativity where-
by,--the older you get, the quicker time seems to fly. You just know the
last decade went by faster than the one before. It gets to the point, the
older you get, even the years and months start going by faster than
those before. When you get old enough, it is the days that seem to fly.
That's when you start looking in the paper every morning, checking the
obits to make sure your name isn't there.

AGE PHASES

Ages 3-21: Time just seems to drag when you are a youngster, you cannot wait to get older, even stretching your age by saying, "I'm almost seven," when you might just be a week or two over your sixth birthday. Isn't is strange how when you're a child you'll sort of fib about your age to make yourself appear older — then at a certain point you might start fibbing to make yourself appear younger?

Your fervor to be older grew when you approached the magic age of 16, giving you wheels, a goal you had been eagerly and impatiently awaiting. What a great feeling — having your own car and not having to be chauffeured around by Mom.

Then you looked forward to 18, when you would graduate and get away from studying (unless you were going on to college.) This was a new independence, being out of school. The only thing is, it definitely became job time to help support your lifestyle and your own car. Of course, you were probably still living and eating at home, and could "borrow" some funds from your folks to aid in your support.

The next magical age was 21, allowing you to vote and be independent! You really are on top of the world! Now you can be your own boss, even if the folks may still be supporting you with funds and while you are living and eating at home. Or, perhaps your folks are funding you big time to go to college. What a great age to reach. No cares, and soon you are going to leave your imprint on society, do some great things — have a lot of great plans. You have such a sense of power and almost immortality.

"Old age may seem a long way off. But on the day it doesn't, it will be too late to do anything about it."

"Youth is not a time of life, it is a state of mind. You are as old as your doubt, your fear, your despair. The way to keep young is to keep your faith young. Keep your self-confidence young. Keep your hope young."
                    — Luella F. Phean

Ages 22-39: The euphoric feeling of power and invincibility lasts until you reach the age of 27, then you start realizing you are nearing "being older." You have become very hesitant about reaching 30, which in your younger days you regarded as almost beyond middle-aged. After passing that 30 mark you still don't look forward to the succeeding years because you know, in the back of your mind, that you are looking toward that dreaded mile-stone of 40, the BIG 4-0!

You need to develop a stock answer to questions you have heard or will hear. You are bound to run into that question from a kid who looks at you and says, "Are you old?" Learn to answer that question with a question: "Compared to what?" It diverts their attention.

Many will start the "age prevarication" and or "age secrecy" mode at this time, thinking they can fool others because they somehow don't think they are showing the signs of aging like others. It is an accomplishment and a certain plateau has been reached when you can lie about your age without laughing. This is beyond me. The truth is, you can have a "baby-face" naturally or by cosmetic surgery, but your hands generally give you away. Until they can do something about the hands you fool nobody but yourself. At this stage what many people want for their birthday is not to be reminded of their age.

When you reach your late 30's and gray hair, wrinkles, less physical activity and other signs of aging show up, it becomes harder to lie about your age. At this time many quit the age prevarication mode and go deeply and completely into the age secrecy mode. In this mode, they would almost rather die than reveal their age. They become very polished in this practice, and will foil any sly attempts to make them reveal their deep secret.

> *"You will always stay young if you live honestly, sleep sufficiently, eat slowly, works industriously, — and lie about your age."*

Ages 39-50 — MIDDLE AGE: This is a traumatic phase in the lives of both men and women. People refer to reaching age 40 as "turning 40." Generally this reference is used with facial expressions almost like you would refer to milk turning sour. This expression, I believe, shows a complete distaste at reaching this milestone.

The Age/Time Relativity really starts kicking in about this time and in no time at all you are picking up speed toward your later years. Now it is much harder to fool people, and your age becomes an even-deeper secret. I actually believe you could fling some people into prison, put them on bread and water, and even torture them, and they would still not reveal their age. It's as if they believe, in spite of all the obvious wrinkles, etc., they still appear to look at least ten years younger than their real age. Many women have made the concealing of their age an art. It has been said that you can't trust a secret to a woman who tells her age, because she will tell anything.

> *"Life begins at 40 — but so do fallen arches, rheumatism, faulty eyesight, and the tendency to tell a story to the same person, three or four times."*
> — William Feather

> *"Middle age: when you're sitting at home on Saturday night and the telephone rings and you hope it isn't for you."* — Ogden Nash

> *"The age of some women is like the speedometer on a used car—you know it's set back but you don't know how far."*

> *"A youthful figure is something you get when you ask a woman her age."*

> *"I refuse to admit that I am more than 52, even if that makes my children illegitimate."*
> — Lady Nancy Astor

THIS IS ABOUT THE TIME YOU WILL FIRST HEAR:
OH, MISTER — OH, SIR — YES, MA'AM: Sometime during this period, you will run into your first experience with a different form of address. The first time you hear it you look around to see who they are talking to. You know you haven't been knighted, so they couldn't possible be talking to you! When you realize they are addressing you, it makes you want to smack them one.

Come to think of it — that's the same thing you used to call older people. It's quite a shocker to find they are addressing you, and you are now one of those older people. You might as well get used to it, because it is a sure sign that you are looking older to those younger than your-self. And besides, what about those old sayings, "Turn-about is fair play?" or "What goes around comes around?"

"A person is always startled when he hears himself seri-ously called old for the first time."
                                           — O. W. Holmes

This is the age when men are worrying about declining sexual per-formance, physical activity, sexual performance, their aging appear-ance, sexual performance, their flabby body, sexual performance, etc. Women are worrying about their wrinkles, appearance, menopause, and their flabby body, sexual performance, etc..

It is hard for both to admit they are no longer a part of the younger generation, and not as strong or athletic as they used to be. They start having minor health problems and have trouble believing a doctor who says they are in good shape—for their age. Isn't it funny how many doctors, after an examination, say this. I suppose they would even say to a 96 year old man who was on his deathbed that, "You are not in bad shape — for your age."

This is also the time that both men and women start having age anx-iety attacks. The feeling of invincibility is now gone and the feeling of mortality replaces it. With some, every chest twinge is a heart attack. They are faced with the realization they are aging, and their once vig-orous strength is waning. It's quite a change and shocker for one who was immortal to find he/she is merely mortal. Age secrecy gets into full swing, thinking perhaps they can keep others from knowing their true age. They may somehow think not only will they fool others, but God as well, and as a result be passed over in the aging process and stay for-ever young. I say, whatever makes them happy.

Many physical changes occur starting at this time or before: graying, baldness (men), dental problems, eyesight, lessened physical ability, etc. You are not as healthy but always think that in a week or two you will be as good as ever. You seem to be doing some things more often during this time: urinating, going to the doctor, going to funerals.

Your bathroom cabinet seems to have accumulated an interesting inventory: Polident, Doan's, suppositories, Grecian Formula, Prozac, zinc hearing aid batteries, blood pressure kit, etc. Also, "alternative medicine" now means Maalox.

"Middle age is when a narrow waist and a broad mind
begin to change places."
— Glenn Dorenbush

Perhaps the most dramatic change, however, is the mental problems referred to as "MID-LIFE CRISIS!":

"MID-LIFE CRISIS!": While we are talking about age phases of our lives, we must talk about "mid-life crisis." What is mid-life crisis? It is that most traumatic time during middle age (usually from 40 - 50.) Something really goes wrong in people's heads when they start having some of the natural signs of growing older: graying hair, male baldness, minor aches, pains and medical problems, hearing and vision loss, dental problems, reduced muscle and limb function, a paunch that can't be flattened, etc. They seem to have the feeling that it isn't long until senility, so live it up!

A tell-tale sign of mid-life crisis is when you see a middle-aged individual — hair dyed, loud clothing and driving a Porsche 911. Many women have felt that when Fred? left her, it would be in a pine box. Instead, he departed in a late model Porsche with a late model bimbo.

Both men and women come to the realization their life is half over, and feel that somehow that isn't enough, and go "dingy." For the want of a better term, they make a complete fool of themselves. They realize their sex life lacks that old "pizzaz" and determine, "No way can it be my my performance that is not up to snuff, it must be my spouse. I need to have a different sex partner, and it will be "wow" again." They convince themselves it will be better with different sex partners.

A women who is affected might leave her loving mate, with or without the kids. Many times, she will have facelift, liposuction, hair color change (to blonde?), breast augmentation, tummy tuck, etc. Often they come on to other men and let them know they are "available", or already have been sleeping with another man.

Men are affected much more dramatically than women by mid-life crisis. They somehow feel they have been cheated in life, and their maleness is threatened, and they just might be impotent soon, so they better get all the use out of that sex tool they can — before it is trashed. They really go 'round the bend. In this phase, the man thinks he is still irresistible to younger women, and sets out to try to prove it. There is no end to the completely asinine things a man will do to humiliate himself, his family, and others while in this crisis.

Generally, the typical man will get his hair dyed and/or a hairpiece for baldness. He will drench himself with some strange fragrance that creates an "aura" around him, purchase an expensive sports car, and dress accordingly. Visualize a loose silky shirt open 3 or 4 buttons down, gold chains, youthful pleated pants, and expensive stylish shoes.

He will either have a "young thing" on the string, or go out "trolling" in his fancy sports car for a much younger female. Many times he will end up leaving an attractive and intelligent wife and family to live with a female half his age, whose deepest mind-broadening reading is Glamor magazine. Would you not doubt his sanity?

"Be wise with speed; a fool at forty is a fool indeed."
— Edward Young

You are now approaching that dreaded, seldom mentioned age — 50! You decide that pushing 50 is exercise enough — you needn't exert any more energy than that. By the fiftieth birthday you are probably on your fourth dog.

At this time, when you enter a room, you seem to start looking for a place to sit down, preferably a chair where it will not be too hard to get up again. This is a time when your friends start to look like they are really aging fast and look much older than you think yourself to be. It is an undeniable fact that it now takes much longer to rest than it did to get tired.

Ages 50's, 60's, 70's & ON: One of the most dreaded "mile-age-markers" we have is the BIG 50 — ONE-HALF OF A CENTURY! Never used to think in terms of being half a century old, did you? Now you are beginning to get in the big time. Many people even decline having a 50th birthday, thinking it won't be as bad if they don't authenticate it with a celebration, and perhaps they could masquerade as a younger person since people won't know.

When you first hit that critical 50, steel yourself — you'll probably get an invitation to join AARP. Another thing, be ready to receive the first mug or T-shirt "Worlds Best or #1 Grandpa/Grandma." Things like this tend to put you into a temporary depressed state if you are not prepared.

You come to realize that the 50's have certain privileges such as joining AARP and getting senior discounts on most everything. There are times, however, when you wish AARP would send "Modern Maturity" in a plain brown envelope. Think about it — the 50's are not so bad. You survived your 40's and now have certain privileges — AARP, an afghan for the shoulders and spending the kids inheritance on liposuction and cruises. You can now start calling wrinkles "laugh lines". Your tactful friends will start putting one candle on your cake — sparing you the effort of blowing out so many.

The late 40's and the 50's is the time when many couples decide to go back to the same location for a second honeymoon. That is great, but a bit of advice: Don't try to do everything you did on the first. Tip the bellhop extra and let him carry her over the threshold. And don't even try to attain the sexual performance of bygone days. Sexual terms have taken on a whole new meaning. "Twice a night" now refers to trips to the bathroom; "performance anxiety" is now referring to your golf game; and "frequency rate" is how often the kids call to borrow money or how often the wife asks you to fix the faucet.

One might ask if they are considered sexy during this phase of life. It would probably depend on your definition of sexy relative to your age. You might be considered by your peers to be a sexy male if you talked more about fishing, golf, gardening, etc., and less about your gallstones, hemorrhoids, etc. You might be considered by your peers to be a sexy female if you talked more about shopping, dining, gardening, etc., and less about your gallstones, hemorrhoids, etc.

By this time, you are probably well into an all-important phase of your life — GRAND-PARENTING! Isn't it great, you can spoil the kids rotten, make brats out of them—and go home when they get on your nerves. You can get all your beauty sleep since they live in a different house. You can also help raise them by sharing advice (welcome or not) with their parents. Now, that is the way to raise kids — no problems!

The biggest thrill is showing everyone that they are the most beautiful and outstanding children in the country. You are not sure, but you think they would do well in a national contest or something. You amass pictures of them doing everything—lying naked on the bed, getting their dirty diaper changed, eating—with food all over the face and in their hair, potty training, etc. You carry this packet of pictures and show them to close friends, not so close friends, and even strangers if you find an opening. You develop the knack of blocking a person's retreat, using a fast-draw of the packet and wowing them with these pictures of your exceptional grandchildren.

I really believe that a new organization should be formed, patterned after AA or Alcoholics Anonymous. It could be called GA or Grandparents Anonymous, for those Grandparents bound and determined to "show and brag." They could have support groups, and general meetings where an individual might get up and say: "My name is ...., and I am a compulsive obsessive Grandparent. I have refrained from this behavior now for a full week, and ....."

This is also the time you start reading the obits regularly with your morning coffee. You are not looking for acquaintances, necessarily, but for the ages of those who have "passed on." You are hoping that all those listed are much older than you — perhaps at least 90 years old.

> *"He's so old that when he orders a three-minute egg,*
> *they ask for the money up front."*
> — Milton Berle

> *"I get up each morning, gather my wits.*
> *Pick up the paper, read the obits.*
> *If I'm not there I know I'm not dead.*
> *So I eat a good breakfast and go back to bed."*
> — Pete Seeger

THIS IS ABOUT THE TIME YOU HEAR:

"YOU'RE SURE LOOKING GOOD": Have you ever heard that phrase? I have — many, many times. I have heard it so often, I considered change my name to that — except it has far too many syllables. It seems the older you get, the more you "look good." At the rate I've been hearing it, I surely am going to look as good as Clark Gable before I die. (OF COURSE I meant as good before Gable died! — Give me a break!)

To reply to that statement, "You're looking good!", I am often tempted to say, "Compared to what, somebody in the intensive care unit?" This is a phrase we are all familiar with, meant as a compliment, but in reality meaning: "You're looking good to have been born before the earth cooled," or "born while the Dead Sea was still alive."

> *"Whenever a man's friends begin to compliment him about looking young, he may be sure that they think he is growing old."*
> — Washington Irving

> *"You've heard of the three ages of man—youth, age, and "you're looking wonderful."*
> — Cardinal Spellman

By this time the Age/Time Relativity is revved up, the course is down-hill, and in no time at all you are picking up speed toward the 60s, then 70's, and beyond. The best answer to give to a youngster who asks "Are you old?" is "Compared to what?"
In your 6O's there are definite signs that people catagorize you as old. They may call at 9 p.m., and ask, "Did I wake you?", or they always jump up from a comfortable chair and offer it to you. It gets sort of embarrassing when a lady gets up and offers you her seat on the bus, like you look old and feeble enough to collapse. You had much rather stand than be embarrassed like that. But, oh well, it is a seat — and that beats standing.

In your 6O's you finally acknowledge that you are among the old. You find it is much easier to do without sex than without your glasses. There's very little left to learn the hard way. It's revealing when you have a party and the neighbors don't even realize it. Your investment in health insurance is really paying off, and people no longer thinks you are a hypochondriac. More and more you are hearing that maddening phrase: "You're sure looking good."
This is about the age when many will have the inclination to live in a gated community and drive a big Caddy, Lincoln or Ford Crown Victoria. If you are a "snowbird", you tend to winter down south in a gated community. You drive your big car in a slow and erratic manner

which will serve to infuriate the natives. I personally saw a bumper sticker on a Florida car which read: "When I Get Old, I Am Going To Move Up North And Drive Slow."

SPEAKING OF LOOKS, ABOUT THIS TIME, YOU NOTICE:
PEOPLE APPEAR TO BE DIFFERENT: Perhaps you're feeling pretty good about yourself and aging, when suddenly you take a good look at your kids, and note they are starting to look middle-aged! That doesn't do anything for your feeling younger, it might even make you feel older.

Have you noticed the strange and eerie thing that has happened? The country is now being operated by professional people who appear to be teenagers, or in their early 20's. Doctors, for instance. You might go to a different doctor and are shown to one of the rooms when it is your turn. In comes a young person who you assume must be a trainee male nurse, because he doesn't look like he shaves yet. He introduces himself as Dr. ...., and you are tempted to ask to see his license. Do you really want this young sprout messing around with your private areas or your insides? It makes you yearn for an old, overweight doctor with a few health problems of his own — one who can really relate to you.

A PERSONAL EXPERIENCE: I was visiting in a hospital room with a brother who was a patient there. In came his doctor, who looked about college age. He wore a white doctor's coat, with a stethoscope in the pocket. I could see, below the white coat, blue-jeans and scuffed Nikes. The next time I was there, he came in for a quick visit, without the smock, wearing a T-shirt with the blue-jeans and Nikes.I wondered if that TV show "Doogie Howser, MD" was patterned after him? He was very efficient and capable, however.

Other professional people look very young. Flying on commercial airlines is scary enough, and it certainly isn't very comforting to board a plane that has a pilot and crew so young looking it gives you the impression this might be a college class project. You yearn for a pilot and co-pilot with some gray hair at the temples at least.

ANOTHER PERSONAL EXPERIENCE: My wife is one who really does not like to fly. On take-offs, she says she never puts all her weight down. We both got nervous on one occasion: We were in Key West and flew home to Missouri and back. We had to take a smaller plane to Miami to catch the main flight. When we boarded this smaller plane (which was full), a lady young enough to be my daughter told me to sit in the co-pilot's seat. She turned out to be the pilot — the only pilot.

On the return trip, we got the same plane and pilot, only this time a rather obese man sat in the co-pilot's seat. The woman in front of us mentioned something about the co-pilot, and I told her the situation. Anyway, this lady seemed very calm — until she de-planed. She then came completely unglued and fell weeping into the welcoming arms of her friends. Would you say the whole situation made her a wee bit upset? (Incidentally, this young female pilot did an excellent flying job.)

> *A couple had been married for 25 years and also celebrated their 60th birthdays. During the celebration a fairy appeared and said that because they had been such a loving couple all those years, she would give them one wish each.*
>
> *The wife said, "I've always wanted to travel around the world." The fairy waved her wand and BOOM — she had the tickets in her hand!*
>
> *Next, it was the husband's turn. He paused for a moment, then said shyly, "Well, I'd like to have a woman 30 years younger than me." The fairy picked up her wand and BOOM — he was 90!*

In your 70's your joints are more reliable than the Weather Service in forecasting changes. This is when you can tell all your secrets to your friends, because they can't remember them either. It is amazing the fascination you now have with the "Obits" in your local paper. The surprising part is that you don't really care who died as long as it isn't you. You are looking mostly for ages, hoping there is not many of your age bracket.

Professional people, doctors, lawyers, airline pilots, etc., all look like they must be participating in a class project, and are not out of school, — even Uncle Sam starts looking young to you. It seems that everything hurts at this age, and what doesn't hurt, simply doesn't work. I have often wondered if it's true that you're only as old as you feel, how in the world can I be alive at 145?

During the years up to this time you have noticed some almost magical changes in technology and events as you sped toward your later years. Just reflect on this: Many of us can say we were before television, atoms, radar, Loran, home computers, flourescent lights, Jeeps, penicillin, polio shots, antibiotics, Scotch tape, nylon, dacron, jet planes, helicopters, FM radio, electric typewriters, DUCT TAPE, W-D 40, velcro, and a host of other things. I have named just a few. Get a pencil and paper and list the others you can think of — on second thought, get a legal pad of paper. Sort of blows your mind when you think of it, doesn't it?

You noticed I put DUCT TAPE & W-D 40 in caps? That's because I consider them to be two of the greatest inventions of the century. Think about it — what would we do without them? The rule for their use is simple: If it moves and shouldn't — use duct tape; if it doesn't move and should — use W-D 40. Wouldn't you agree they are as handy as the pocket on a shirt?

We were privileged to have 5 & 10 cent stores where you could actually buy things for 5 and 10 cents. My fondest memories are of the ice cream fountains and parlors where you could enjoy a wide selection of ice cream concoctions. Brings back pleasant memories, doesn't it?

One reassuring thing at this time of life is that many of the things you buy now are a good investment — they are not likely to wear out in your lifetime. Isn't that great?

Most of all, we have experienced some rather rapid changes in ourselves and others as we sped through the aging process. Let's look at some of these changes in a random fashion:

> *"Old age is no place for sissies."*
> — Bette Davis

> *"We do not quit playing because we grow old; We grow old because we quit playing."*
> — Oliver W. Holmes

WATTLES & WRINKLES

Mirror, Mirror on the wall,
Can this be me, wattles, wrinkles & all?

"There is hope for anyone who can look in a mirror and laugh at what he sees."

"There is always a lot to be thankful for if you take time to look for it. For example, I am sitting here thinking how nice it is that winkles don't hurt."

FACIAL WATTLES: Wattles seem to happen slowly but surely. One day you might look in the mirror and find they are fully developed wattles of fatty skin hanging from your jowls — think turkey! They do seem to get more pronounced as time goes by. Very little research has been done in regard to the care and treatment of wattles. Perhaps, the only answer for wattles and double chin is corrective surgery!

FACIAL WRINKLES: Wrinkles seem to appear suddenly as crows-feet near the eyes and mouth and spread their way outward. This problem is exacerbated by the sun rays you soak up. You sometimes pay for all those nice tans, with a wrinkled, pebbly skin that could only sexually arouse an alligator or lizard. You know you have a real problem when a fortune teller offers to read your face. That can be very embarrassing. It is common to start laboring under the impression that "laugh-lines" are distinguished looking.

BODY WRINKLES: You just can't win as far as your body is concerned: When you are old and slim, you generally have many wrinkles. If you are old and fat — you generally have folds. It's embarrassing to try to straighten out the wrinkles in your socks — and realize you are not wearing any!

THE BATTLE AGAINST FACIAL WRINKLES:
COSMETIC SKIN CARE: The demand for "magical" cosmetic skin products have made some cosmetic companies very rich. People buy

huge amounts of their "make you look young again" products to combat wrinkles. This does help your skin, but does not stop the aging process. Time marches on, wrinkles multiply and deepen; and face cream, powder and other cosmetic products collect in those wrinkles, sometimes falling out in little chunks.

Many women tend to use a tad too much mascara and other cosmetics. One example that readily comes to mind is Tammy Faye Baker. After watching her go into a crying jag on TV, my advice to women who model their make-up after her is to avoid sad movies, funerals and weddings. And don't get caught in the rain without an umbrella. Remember Tammys's tear stained and mascara streaked face. Not a pretty sight! — think chocolate mascara pie. A sight not pleasant to behold, it makes me shudder just to think of it.

Let's face one fact at this stage in life: it takes twice as long to look half as good.

> *"All of those formulas for staying young will be totally unsuccessful until they learn how to iron out a few wrinkles."*

COSMETIC SURGERY/FACELIFT: This time of life is sometimes referred to as the "Wonder Years" — you wonder why you didn't save for a facelift! Cosmetic doctors get big bucks and drive Porshes for this procedure. They lop some skin off, stretch what's left to the sides to attempt to hide the scars. This smooths the skin for a time, but wrinkles have a way of returning with more age, so it must be repeated, perhaps more than once — sending doctors into a higher tax bracket. Eventually, your eye sockets and mouth get pulled to the sides so much it gives you a thin-lipped Oriental look.

Many stage and movie stars have had this done so often, you wonder if they couldn't use Velcro to make it simpler. However, I guess it would show, wouldn't it? Those who have plastic surgery often are examples of people with mis-matched parts. It's strange to see a youthful face on a person who can't bend over to tie their shoes.

There are many things you can dip into your kid's college fund to pay for. Consider a complete face lift (fuller lips, new chin, etc.), or eyes done, nose job, neck tightened, hair plugs, bosom implants, calf implants, love handles sucked and hip reduction among the most important.

"Age should not have its face lifted, but it should rather teach the world to admire wrinkles as the etchings of experience and the firm line of character."
                                          — Ralph B. Perry

MY FREE "NO-FAIL" SUGGESTION: I have a sure-fire, cost-free, non-patented, guaranteed, and ENJOYABLE method to rid yourself of wrinkles. It is very simple, and the beauty of it is—anyone can enjoy doing it. Eat lots of good tasting stuff and get FAT! Obesity is sure to work. Many older people put on weight anyway, but wouldn't it be fun to really pork it down? With the final result of obesity, it is guaranteed that your wrinkles will be gone. Side effects will include folds instead of body wrinkles, and an addition to your facial wattles making them rounder and smoother.

Prove the validity of this method by answering this question: "Have you ever seen wrinkles on a balloon?"

"The common foible of women who have been hand-some is to forget that they are no longer so."
                                          — Rochefoucauld

A middleaged woman had a heart attack and was taken to the hospital. While on the operating table she had a near-death experience. Seeing God, she asked if this was it. God said, "No, you have another 43 years, 2 months and 8 days to live".

Upon recovery, she decided to stay in the hospital and have a facelift, liposuction, breast augmentation, tummy tuck, etc. She even had her hair color changed. Since she had so much more time to live, she figured she might as well make the most of it.

She left the hospital after the last operation and while crossing the street was struck down by an ambu-lance speeding to the hospital.

Arriving in front of God, she demanded, "I thought you said I had another 40 years?"

God answered, "I didn't recognize you."

HAIR TO THE CROWN

GRAYING

*Mirror, Mirror on the wall,
I'm just too young for any gray hair at all!*

Age is really sneaky. It creeps up on you like cheap underwear. Gray hair is one of the first indications you are getting along in age, but can happen in your 30's. You are sailing along, thinking you will always look young and full of vim and vinegar. One day, you look in the mirror, perhaps shaving or applying cosmetics. You notice an alien thing in your fine head of hair. It can't be! — but it is — a gray hair! You examine closely and find there are more. You immediately get the tweezers, pluck those darn things out. The idea — you are too young for grey hair and must rid your head of this evidence.

Perhaps 2 or 3 weeks go by, and again you look in the mirror. Oh, no! You see grey hairs again, only more this time. You are determined, so you pluck or pull those. Later on, when more appear, even more numerous, you give up. You know that plucking them is not the answer, because you could pluck yourself bald.

THE REMEDY: The only answer to eliminating gray, of course, is to dye it. That however, brings up another problem. People should not be allowed to pick their color or even shade of color. It should be a law that you must consult with and have a professional (with good taste) dye your hair. For instance: You see men and women who seem to think if dark hair is good, the blackest black is better — even though it might be atop an apparently old face that is a mass of wrinkles. You see others who seem to think blonde hair is nice with their wrinkles.

You even see some women who prefer the brightest off-color red you can imagine. Why? I don't know. It sure isn't a natural color — God has better taste than that. My first inclination is to throw water on them, or throw them on the ground and roll them in a blanket, to put out the flames.

"Pull out a gray hair and seven will come to its funeral."
— Pennsylvania Dutch

"Nothing is more quiet than the sound of hair going grey."

"Though gray be your hair
With little to part
This does not denote
The age of your heart."
— Michael Franklin Ellis

MALE BALDNESS

Mirror, Mirror on the wall,
I'm awful young for my hair to fall!

"No man should fret in case his hair
Turns silver in his prime
He's fortunate that some was there
To turn at turning time."
— William W. Pratt

Hair loss is a common problem that comes with growing old, but can start when reasonably young. It can be a genetic thing. Baldness is a big vanity thing with many men. There will be those who secretly read brochures on "Hair Club for Men", and even start getting bids on hair implants. I must say that some have a lot of courage — being bald on top and sporting a pony-tail.

Many have made a healthy bank account playing on the vanity of baldness. They have brought out, over time, many gadgets and numerous concoctions and products that are promised to magically grow hair — and many men have tried them all in their desperate quest for hair. So far, that magic potion has not been invented, and the only thing those concoctions now on the market have helped is the bank account of those selling them. Still, with all this past experience, men are ready and eager to buy the next new "magical hair restorer" that hits the market.

"There's one thing about baldness — it's neat."

"There are three ways in which a man can wear his hair: parted, un-parted, departed."

SOME "REMEDIES" FOR BALDNESS ARE:

THE "COMB-OVER": The reason I call this the comb-over is obvious. Many men try to make their remaining side hair (normally their sideburns) cover the baldness. They lower their part to just above the ear, let that hair grow quite long and comb it over toward the other side of the head. To them it seems to look natural and realistic. Looks are obviously in the eyes of the beholder, because to others it looks like thin side hair combed over a "fly and mosquito landing zone." Or perhaps according to how one oils it, it looks like a large many-legged spider on the side of the head. Sometimes, it appears to be a very flimsy hairpiece that is slipping off the side of the head.

The major problem with this comb-over is that you must always pay strict attention to the wind direction and act accordingly. There are certain rules to follow: You must sit with your part to the windward side, and you must walk with your part to the windward side — even if you have to walk backwards. If this is not done, the wind has a tendency to do some embarrassing things with your hair. It will lift your hair and turn it back in the other direction — putting it over your ear and perhaps almost to your shoulder. You will have to excuse people who stare in fascination at this activity.

The only thing that might help the comb-over is to oil or grease it to keep it anchored down in a breeze. But this does enhance the huge spider look on your bald head. It has its other problems, too, as it tends to attract more flies and mosquitos, and the glare from reflected light blinds bystanders unless they don their sunglasses.

HAIR TRANSPLANT: This is an extreme, expensive and painful method. It is expensive — and afforded only by those people who are mad at their money, or as we say in the Ozarks, "have enough money to burn a wet mule."

The procedure is simple, but very painful: They remove plugs of hair from somewhere else and transplant it to your head. I don't know if they have to fertilize it or not. I know of some people who probably would have enough fertilizer up there anyway. Eventually it does take root, although it takes a long time. Now this is just my personal opinion—I think it looks like hair transplanted from somewhere else.

THE HAIRPIECE: The hairpiece is the answer to male baldness, but it also carries it's own major problems. First, good hairpieces are expensive, but can be worth it if you have the money. All too many men think any hairpiece will do — why spend big bucks? As a result, they wear hairpieces that you could spot from Mars. There are a number of men who fall into this category, and they could form a Bad Hairpiece Club — with a huge membership.

Some hairpieces are so obviously cheap they resemble a furry critter more than real hair. You even wonder if some are recycled and dyed "road-kill." Definitely a money saver as it would only require gas money and time to acquire a fresh one. If lucky you might even be able to kill your own for a brand new fluffy look.

One thing is for sure: a tasteless hairpiece will change the way people look at you— often with a quick double-take to be sure their eyes aren't fooling them.

Mirror, Mirror on the wall,
I'm awful young for my hair to fall!

HAIR, HAIR!
— EYEBROWS, NOSTRILS & EARS

Mirror, Mirror on the wall,
Lots of hairs, but plucking them out makes me squall!

God must have a sense of humor. No matter how much hair you lose off your head, most males start growing it like bad weeds on the eyebrows and in the nostrils and ears. It is strange that men are very aware and will do extreme things about the hair or lack thereof on the head, but remain completely oblivious to it growing wildly out of other locations. Some get to the point of having hair growing out the ears and nostrils that makes them look as if they have worn out shaving brushes stuck in them. Actually, for many men, bald or not, a "bad hair day" could refer to ear and nostril hair.

If you do try to take care of nostril hair — use scissors, or preferably have your barber do so. Tweezers, take it from me, are not the answer — it does bring tears to your eyes—very painful! A strange place a single "wild" hair or two will grow is on top of the ear. This is an interesting focal point for people to stare at when talking to you.

Shaggy eyebrows have their own particular problem, besides getting to look like worn out and mashed scrub brushes. There are always at least one or two really "wild" hairs on each brow. They grow very fast and in the most unusual directions. This is very distracting to others.

"I feel so bad for Uncle Ted,
    There's not much hair upon his head.
And, what is worse, he barely hears.
    There's too much hair inside his ears."
                                    — Bruce Lansky

MY BODY IS MY CASTLE —
WHAT A DUMP!

Mirror, Mirror on the wall,
This is not the body I recall!

*"It's not the fact that all my hair
is jumping ship in droves,
or that I hoard my medicines
like precious treasure troves.*

*It's not that once-true memory banks
will not cooperate,
or parts that once had muscle tone
now downward gravitate.*

*It's not the fact that I can't eat
the foods I used to love.
It's not a single one of these —
it's all of the above."*

— Robert Scotellaro

It seems to hit you all of a sudden. You go along thinking you have a pretty fair "bod," and then it happens, perhaps in this way: You take a shower, dry off, walk by a full-length mirror to get your clothing. You glance into the mirror at your side-view, then take a full shot, and you are dismayed by what you see. What has happened to that fine body of just a few short years ago? You did have a good physique, what happened to it? You still have everything you had 20 years ago, but it's a lot lower and misshapen. You can turn sideways, front and back — the view doesn't get any better. The only answer I know is to quit looking in the mirror except in dim light, or get yourself a custom-made trick mirror that makes you look good.

Your physical capabilities are quite obvious when your wife has to start helping you put on your socks, trim your toenails and pick up things you drop. A word of advice: Don't start pointing at the things you want picked up — that leads to a state of high irritation on her part. The final straw is when she offers to change a flat.

Your sense of values change at this time. You used to pick up any coin you spotted on the ground with a sense of elation. Now, you won't bend over for less than a dollar.

> *A woman walked up to a little old man rocking in a chair on his porch.*
>
> *"I couldn't help noticing how happy you look," she said. "What's your secret for a long happy life?"*
>
> *"Well, honey, I smoke three packs of cigarettes a day," he said. "I also drink a case of whiskey a week, eat fatty foods, and never exercise."*
>
> *"That's amazing, "the woman said. "How old are you?"*
>
> *"Twenty-six," he said.*

"I finally got my head together, now my body is falling apart."

"I have a million dollar figure but it's all loose change!"

"I'm wrinkled, saggy, lumpy, — and that's just my left leg."

"Careful grooming and a smooth paint job will take 20 years off a woman's true age. But you can't fool a long flight of stairs."

Mirror, Mirror on the wall,
Who's got the biggest and flabbiest butt of all?

THE "FULL-FIGURED" BODY

Mirror, Mirror on the wall,
Who's got the biggest and flabbiest butt of all?

*"Eat, drink and be merry — and tomorrow you'll wish
you were dead."*

It is a strange "law of aging": The older you get, the harder it is to
lose weight. Your body and your fat become really good friends. Your
appetite for food increases and your appetite for exercise decreases.
You might say that extra weight is sneaky, because it comes up on you
from the rear.

A good indication of extra weight is when every thing jiggles —
even your upper arms. There is a new meaning to some terms: "hip-
huggers" could be referring to cellulite and "hanging out" could mean
the protuberance over your belt.

There comes a time in your life when you quit trying to suck in your
stomach, no matter who walks into the room. If you think for one
moment that "old soldiers fade away," just try getting into your old uni-
form. This can be rather dangerous — you can get a hernia trying to
button or zip your pants.

It seems when you get older your metabolism and calorie require-
ments slow down at about the same rate that your appetite picks up.
Some with special genes do enter old age slim, some too slim, but most
of us regular folks don't. All those Oreos, Twinkies, ice cream, etc. are
stored in the most obvious and inconvenient places. Anyway, the older
you get, the tougher it is to lose weight because by then your body and
your fat are really the best of friends. One of the mysteries of life at this
stage is how a person can eat a two pound box of chocolates and gain
five pounds — can you figure?

They say you can trust a fat man — he will not stoop to anything.
Believe me, the "full-figured" person courts danger just to tie his shoes
or put on his socks. You cut off your blood and air supply, blood rush-
es to your head, and you get pretty light-headed. It's even possible to
pass out. That alarms your spouse until they get used to it.

If you have a paunch and arthritis you want to bring the no-socks
rage back into style, and you prefer slip on shoes. It's almost impossi-

ble to tie your shoes, or even put on socks, without feeling like you are about to give birth.

While we are on the subject, I want to get something off my chest. Don't you just hate it when some skinny person says, in a simpering voice, "I don't have a lot of appetite. Why, sometimes I even forget to eat." GIVE ME A BREAK! Now I have forgotten my car, my car keys, my wife's name, but I NEVER, NEVER have forgotten to eat! You must have a special brand of stupidity to forget to eat. Doesn't that really frost you?

THE REMEDY FOR EXTRA WEIGHT?: There are four options one can use to handle the problem of extra weight. They are listed from the least popular to the most popular, with D being the most chosen option:

A. LIPOSUCTION: This is very expensive — several hundred bucks per thigh or buttock, I would say. The only problem with liposuction is that it doesn't change your eating habits and your body starts storing those Twinkies, Oreos, etc. in your thighs and buttocks again. You have to return again and again to get that storage of fat sucked out. After a time, people generally run out of incentive or money, or both at the same time.

B. VIGOROUS EXERCISE: I know it would be good to do bends and touch your toes — personally, I decided long ago that if God had wanted me to touch my toes, he would have put them much higher — say about my kneecaps. Weight-lifting would be good, but my idea of weight lifting is just to stand up — it takes me two tries to get up from the couch.

Jogging is also good exercise, though it can be very hazardous. There are those whose thighs rubbed together so much they caught their underwear on fire. That is dangerous.

C. DIETING: A diet is the least popular, though tried and abandoned by almost all people. There are many diets and diet products on the market. Personally, I think a diet is a brief period of starvation followed by an immediate increase in the original weight.

I would propose one structured diet that may have a chance of working. Put the one who wants to lose weight in a brightly lighted room, and allow them to eat anything they wish. The only stipulation, the room must be full of naked obese people. It could be called the "grossed out diet." Do you think it has possibilities?

D. FORGET IT!: Forget the whole thing and learn to be jolly, fulfilling the old myth that all fat people are jolly. Buy clothing that fits your figure and bras that fasten in the front and live with it.

> *"I've been on a constant diet for the last two decades.*
> *I've lost a total of 78) pounds. By all accounts, I should*
> *be hanging from a charm bracelet."*
> — Erma Bombeck

VANITY, VANITY, THY NAME IS VANITY— CLOTHING AND THE "FULL FIGURE"

Mirror, Mirror on the wall,
Now they're making my size way too small!

More than ample bodies bring a major problem in buying clothing, for both men and women:

CLOTHING, MEN: An overweight man should not be allowed to shop for himself. He probably knows better, but vanity will make him ask the clerk for clothing at least one or two sizes too small. It's embarrassing for a clerk to ask you what size undershorts you are looking for, and you vainly ask for 38's. The clerk, looking you up and down with a smirk on his face, says: "Did you want them gift-wrapped?"

A little tip for those men who insist on buying their clothes too small. The best way to put on those shorts, jeans or pants is to lay down on the bed, suck in, have someone assist you — and hope the button doesn't pop and injure the eye of the person helping you.

CLOTHING, WOMEN: Full-figured women should also be required to have a practical person go along to insist they buy the correct size in clothing. They seem to go one way or another. Some tend to buy a large unbelted, loose dress that looks to have been made on special order by Omar the tentmaker. They believe this to be less revealing of their figure. It might indeed hide their figure, but eyes are drawn to what appears to be a tent moving down the street.

Others favor too-small clothing that looks like it's eating them up, or perhaps were melted and poured into it. This really gives them a strange walk, like a marionette. This sort of clothing will not let them bend, squat, or sit down very fast for fear something will give. My advice, ladies, is to try something with more give than jeans — how about something fashionable in polyester?

"The cardiologit's diet: If it tastes good, spit it out."

I KEEP MY BODY IN GOOD SHAPE— (ROUND IS A SHAPE!)

Mirror, Mirror on the wall,
Oh, how I used to throw a ball!

Ever noticed, how the older one gets, the better athlete one was in one's youth? Have you ever noticed former youthful athletic ability increases with age? The continued telling and expanding on the truth convinces the teller it is real. For instance, an oldster was laying some brags on a friend of mine who happened to have gone to the same high school, but not in the same year. It seems this fella claimed to be a great football player, and even captain of the team. My friend couldn't remember what he looked like in high school, so he decided he would look him up in his old high-school yearbook. Well, he found him, but he wasn't the captain of the football team — in fact, he wasn't even on the football team! People can vividly remember some things that never happened.

It is natural to remember how robust you were years ago, but keep this in mind: You have everything now that you had then, only now it's lower, slower and tends to hurt and ache easily. Back then, you were on the go much of the time, but now your back goes out more than you do. You used to be wild and fast in the car, and warned to slow down by the authorities — now the doctors are warning you to slow down for a different reason.

I've always heard that we need to "keep in touch" with our bodies. I don't know what kind of communication they mean, but I sure did hear from mine. Just the other day I said, "Body, how about me and you getting up at 6 AM and jogging for three miles every morning to get us in shape." Clear as a bell my body said, "listen you bonehead ... do it and you die with excruciating pain." I have come to the conclusion that I am not into working out or vigorous exercise. My motto: "No Pain, No Pain."

You used to have strong lungs with lasting "wind" in athletics. Now, with age, it gets to the point you can get winded playing chess or dialing long distance. A good test for your wind-power is to put the right number of candles on you next birthday cake and try to blow them out without passing out. It becomes impossible, doesn't it?

Let's get specific about sports and exercise and what you can and cannot do when older.

SPORTS/ATHLETICS: The mind is tricky — it makes decisions your body doesn't agree with. If you think you will try a little one on one basketball with a person approximately one-half your age, take my advice — forget it! He will eat your lunch and your body will regret it. Never let your mind write a check that your body can't cash. If you barge ahead, your body will make you suffer for it. Make the upper age limit about six or seven before you engage in athletic competition with them, and even then, be cautious.

You can always fool people about your athletic ability by wearing a warm-up suit for events like grocery shopping and keeping a tennis racket prominently displayed in your car.

> *"A man's not old when his hair turns grey,*
> *And a man's not old when his teeth decay;*
> *But he's on his way to that final sleep,*
> *When his mind makes appointments his body can't keep."*

THROWING, for example: Remember when you were young, and could throw a football or baseball with ease and power, and you could skip a rock across the water many times? Even though you are much older now, that idea is still imbedded in you mind. Let's say you are walking by a playground, and a baseball comes rolling up toward you. A kid yells, "Hey, mister, would you throw it back, please?" You pick up the ball, your mind saying, "Easy as pie, no problem," but your body is pleading, "No, no! Either roll it to the kid, or let him retrieve his own ball." Your mind ignores this plea and you draw back and heave the ball, in a form that resembles a girls throw. The ball bounces about one-half the way to the kid. Excruciating pain! You realize, with tears in your eyes, your arm will not be up to throwing again until the next decade.

> *"The aging process has you firmly in its grasp if you never get the urge to throw a snowball."*
> — Doug Larson

JUMPING, for instance: It doesn't seem that long ago you could really jump—over the tennis net with ease, for instance. If thinking back makes you want to try it again — Get It Out Of Your Mind! It really isn't a pretty sight to see a former athlete lying flat on his face, all twisted and tangled in a tennis net. With age it gets progressively worse until you are lucky to clear a rope lying on the ground, much less one holding up a tennis net.

AEROBICS & EXERCISE: At a certain age, your mind and body just quit working in harmony and doing things together. "Keeping in shape" is one example of this conflict. Your mind decides you need to tone your body and regain that youthful vigor. Your mind, says "No pain, no gain,"and makes commitments at a health club.

After the first session, when the body shows you what real pain is, your mind starts coming around to agree with the body. Your mind starts saying, "No pain, no pain." Just one or two sessions and your mind waves the white flag to surrender and both say, "Pooh on exercise — down with Jane Fonda!" From that point on, you have subconsciously decided to get your exercise by acting as a pallbearer for friends who did exercise vigorously. I have come to the decision that when I get the urge to exercise — I will just lie down until the feeling passes.

While we are talking about Jane Fonda, let's discuss something I personally would not do. I would not go to one of those gyms where they wear those tight outfits and do aerobics. In the first place, I don't do aerobics, my body is sore enough without putting it through more torture. In the second place, I would be the laughing-stock of the county if I were to don some of those stretchy tights. The only ones that have the physique to wear those outfits and not look like a joke are people who don't need to exercise . Come to think of it, I think that's the reason they do go — to show off their trim bodies.

Don't get me wrong, exercise is good for you I am sure. I am a firm believer in exercise — if you exercise every day you will die healthier. If you are going to exercise, it is best to do it early in the morning before your brain realizes what your body is up to. Did you know that statistics say that every minute you spend exercising, you add a minute to your life? That should give you some real incentive. I put a pencil to that and did some figuring: — that means you can spend at least an extra 5 to 6 months in a care center at $5,000 to $6,900 per month.

I was advised to join a health club to lose weight and get in shape. That was a waste of $500. Some time passed and I didn't lose weight (in fact, gained some) nor did I get in any better shape. I called to complain and was told I actually had to show up, so I gave up that idea.

I personally endorse a good regimen of exercise. First you do lifting exercises — lifting yourself out of your easy chair. Then you take a good walk — from your chair to the dining table, where you do lowering exercises by lowering yourself with gusto into a dining chair. Then you start the arm raises, elbow and wrist bends, fingers strongly holding a fork or spoon with food on it. After a strenuous period of this exercise, you should take a walk — back to the easy chair, lowering your body gently to complete the exercise cycle. This regimen can be followed three or even four times daily, with some in-between walks to the fridge to really "build" that body.

"One reason to smile is that every seven minutes of every day, someone in an aerobics class pulls a hamstring."

"You know you're into middle age when first you realize that caution is the only thing you care to exercise."
                                                    — Charles Ghigna

"I believe every human has a finite number of heartbeats. I don't intend to waste any of mine running around doing exercises."
                                                    — Neil Armstrong

JOGGING: Jogging was really the rage a very few years ago, both for the young and old. It was common to see great numbers of joggers everywhere: in parks, by streets and highways, and even in mall parking lots. According to weather and climate the dress varied from sweats to brightly colored running shorts and tank top, wrist and head sweatbands, and of course expensive running shoes.

Today the scene has changed. The dress is the same, but the number of joggers has declined. Many of the younger and a majority of the older joggers found the cost of orthopedic surgery prohibitive and the rotund ones dreaded the possibility of a heart attack. As the ranks declined, very few old joggers remain and they have developed their own very unique style.

They seem to lean forward at a dangerous angle, flail their arms (resembling someone with a spastic disorder) and move forward with a fast shuffle step. They have to move with this fast step to keep from falling flat on their face. Apparently, a determined look and excessive arm action adds to their feeling of healthy activity.

WALKING: Walking is great, and recommended by virtually all doctors. Anybody will feel better if they walk daily. It is also good for losing weight, and toning up your body muscles.

People, especially older ones, have taken this simple healthful exercise and embellished it to the point of being ludicrous. First, the OUTFITS: You wear shorts and/or sweats, all brightly colored and coordinated. You must have bright head and wrist sweat-bands. Optional but preferred are wrist and ankle weights (especially for oldsters.) A visor and a Sony Walkman with earphones are a must.

The ACTION is the ingredient that makes this walking both interesting and comical. You stiffen your arms and legs and pump them violently, meanwhile leaning forward like you are walking into a gale wind. It appears that you are having a serious problem with your central nervous system causing spasms or seizures and on the verge of collapse. This is the basic style, but there are innumerable interesting variations seen.

Personally, I think this would make a good spectator sport, though perhaps not an Olympic event. I would personally pay to watch it. This would also serve to encourage walkers to compete and get them away from the roadsides. They should be banned from the roads anyway. Distracted drivers are running off the road into embankments or trees or into the oncoming lane of traffic, sometimes causing head-on collisions.

"The only reason I would take up jogging is so I could hear heavy breathing again."
> — Erma Bombeck

"You have to stay in shape. My grandmother started walking five miles a day when she was 60. She's 97 today and we don't know where she is."

GOLF: Golf seems to be the sport of choice for most oldsters. It's good for your health in that you are outside getting a great tan, instead of laying on the couch at home, swigging a brew, and watching Tiger Woods on the TV. Don't expound too much that golf is good exercise, however, because you are not fooling most people, unless they are from Bangladesh. People know that you use those very comfortable golf carts and ride around to your ball, getting as close as possible to keep the walking to a bare minimum. You mostly exercise your arms swinging at the ball and pulling yourself in and out of the golf cart. You also do elbow, wrist and arm exercises by popping a cap and swigging a brew as you are riding down the fairway. Oh, by the way, golf enables men to wear the wildest colored pants imaginable. I actually think the reason most play the game is to wear clothes they would not be caught dead in otherwise. It's a tough sport, isn't it?

"You Couldn't Ruin A Game Like That!"
John and his friend George go golfing together one Saturday morning, as they have done for 24 years straight. Yes, you might say these guys were fanatics about their golfing.

Later that day, John returns home exhausted, and plops down in the easy chair. His wife is concerned and asks if something went wrong with his game.

"No, no," he replied, "I had the best game I had in years! As a matter of fact, I started out the first three holes at 4 under par, including a hole-in-two on the 3rd."

"So why are you so beat?" his wife asked.

"Well, George had a heart attack and died on the 4th hole," he said.

"What?!? And you're so exhausted from trying to save him, huh?"

"No, It was very quick and there was nothing anyone could've done. But after that, it was just hit the ball, drag George, hit the ball, drag George ... "

GENERAL BODY ACTIONS & STUFF

You learn terms relating to your body and its actions that you were not familiar with in your younger days. Think wrinkles, crows feet, gray hair, cellulite, age spots, droop, sag, nagging backache, heartburn, etc. Anymore, the term "alternative medicine" refers to Maalox. "Hip huggers" now refers to cellulite.

You start to stiffen up and this condition of flexibility has various effects. Bending over to touch your toes or even tie your shoes becomes very difficult. Slip-on shoes become your favorite.

It is rather demeaning when your wife offers to change a flat tire.

Your sense of values change — you have to spot $1 or more on the sidewalk before you try to bend over to pick it up. Many men are even affected in their arms — causing them to have problems reaching for the dinner check.

At this age your eating habits change. You find that "Substance Abuse" could refer to using garlic or eating sweet and sour pork. "O. D." means that garlic you love to eat has turned on you.

SITTING BULL

Mirror, Mirror on the wall,
Let me sit before I fall!

Believe it or not, sitting is a major concern in the life of the older person. As soon as they enter a house or room they are looking for a place to sit. Didn't you used to get amused at "old people" trying to find a place to sit, checking chairs out? Now that you are one of those old people, you realize why they were looking. Not only were they looking for a comfortable chair, they are looking for a certain kind of comfortable chair. Their main concern is finding a chair they can get out of without assistance, and without making unseemly noises. It is very demoralizing and embarrassing, but it always happens—at the moment you rise and make those noises the room happens to be very quiet. Not a person in the room misses the show you are putting on for their benefit. They pretend not to notice, but you see some cough to cover their laughter.

Another problem is a hammock. It is real easy to get in a hammock — the problem is in trying to climb out of one. It can get pretty hairy and you might end up looking like a contortionist, or a human pretzel.

PARTY, PARTY, PARTY!

Mirror, Mirror on the wall,
Please give me an evening that is dull.

Weren't those the days, when you wanted to go, go, go and party, party, party? Put it in your memory book, because they aren't coming back. That was then, this is now. You might still want to burn the midnight oil, but it lasts only as long as you do—until about 9:00 PM. Now when you refer to "tying one on" — likely your are referring to fastening you Medic Alert bracelet.

Remember how all your neighbors used to complain about your wild parties. Let's face it, now you can have a wild party and your closest neighbors won't even notice. In fact, it gets to the point where you appear in your pajamas and even start flicking lights as hints for your guests to leave.

In your younger days, you used to "paint the town red" almost every day. It's different now, isn't it?-- it requires a very long rest before you can apply a second coat. Now, your idea of a night out is to sit on the patio. Even your idea of "happy hour" now is an afternoon nap.

The older you get, the more you really look forward to a dull evening. In fact, even Bingo becomes more and more fascinating and becomes your "living it up" time. Isn't it funny how different it used to be than it is now? When you go on vacation now, your energy runs out before your money does. As to sex, "frequency rate" now means how often the kids call to borrow money or the wife asks you to fix the faucet.

"You're getting old when you don't care where your wife goes, just so you don't have to go along."

A Jewish lady, 68 years old, went to the doctor for a checkup. The doctor told her she needed more activity and recommended sex three times a week. She says "You better tell my husband." The doctor goes out in

the waiting room and tells the husband that his wife
needs to have sex three times a week.
The husband, 70 years old, says "Which days?"
The doctor says, "Monday, Wednesday and Friday."
The Jewish husband says, "Vell, I can bring her
Monday and Wednesday, but Friday she'll have to take
the bus."

BODILY "FUNCTIONS"

Mirror, Mirror on the wall,
Whose latest BM is the most interesting of all?

POOPING: Isn't it strange how some things go full circle? For instance, a child of a certain age (1 - 2 years old) gets great satisfaction and a sense of accomplishment in pooping. Later, this same child is allowed to pick a cereal at the store, and chooses his cereal for the toy inside. As the child grows, those things are forgotten — until he gets old. Then he (or she) will get great satisfaction and a sense of accomplishment in—pooping! For the final irony, they now choose their cereals for the fiber inside instead of a toy. They have become supporters of movements—by eating bran, prunes and raisins.

He/she is so proud of their accomplishment, they will discuss it with other oldsters, sort of comparing notes on what helps their pooping, and talking about cereals from which they get fiber. That is rather distasteful but no big problem. The major problem is—they many times will have this discussion in restaurants or other public places. They generally discuss it very loudly, supposedly so others can hear and share in the joy of their accomplishment.

URINATING, MEN: Your wife, like all other females, probably had to pee so often that you perhaps teased her about being a charter member of the P.E.O. Club (Pee Every Opportunity.) You used to have great control and when you did have to pee, it would be a good strong controlled stream.

I used to tease my wife about being a charter member of the "P.E.O. Club." Now, on trips you stop at several rest stops (at least half of them), and you are just as ready to pee as your wife. Unless you drink more, or take water pills, you don't pee any more volume — just often er. You have adopted a new maxim: "Never pass up an opportunity to pee." There is something strange about traveling on the Interstate: when you see a sign that says "No Services" at a rest stop, your bladder really activates and goes into a panic state.

It isn't a strong steady stream anymore — more like a weaker dribble-stream . You remember in high school basketball, the coach would tell you to control your dribble. Oh, do we need him now, coaching us on how to control our dribble. Anyway, at those rest stops, you have to stand close to the urinal and be patient. If you don't stand close, you might pee on your shoes or the lower pants leg.

You have to be patient, because your "pee-thing" seems to have a mind of its own. It will make you think your bladder is empty, hesitate awhile, and then give a final little squirt. This can cause embarrassing situations. For instance, sometimes men are waiting in line behind you to use the urinals. This, of course, puts pressure on you to hurry, so you do. Thinking you are done, you zip up your pants. Almost every time just as you zip up your pants, that ornery "pee-thing" will put a little squirt in your pants, making a wet spot that is very obvious and embarrassing.

What to do? You are not agile enough to put one foot on the wall above the blow dryer, and others would stare at you if you could. It's also too embarrassing to remove your pants and hold them up to the dryer — again others would stare. There is only one course of action walk back to your car, with your hands or a paper held casually over your groin area. If you make it back to your car without too many people snickering, you still have one major obstacle — your wife! There is never any luck there, however, because she always checks to see if you forgot to zip your pants. You just can't win!

> *"It doesn't matter how much you shake it and dance,*
> *The last few drops end up in your pants!"*

> *"First you forget names, then you forget faces, then*
> *you forget to pull your zipper up, then you forget to*
> *pull your zipper down."*   — Leo Rosenberg

BODY PARTS & FACULTIES

Mirror, Mirror on the wall,
My teeth, eyes and hearing — they're beyond recall!

TEETH: It's a natural thing to lose one's teeth as you grow old, though it can be faster with poor dental care. Many people have dentures, or at least bridgework, before they are through middle age. Good, well-fitting and natural looking dentures are a boon to those who have lost their teeth for whatever reason. Note that the key words are: "good, well-fitting" and "natural looking."

Mirror, Mirror on the wall,
My teeth, eyes and hearing — they're beyond recall!

I don't know why it is, but some dentures are made in such a way that they "whistle" when people talk through them. I have been entertained often by people who, when talking excitedly, whistle a tune sounding similar to "Yankee Doodle" through their teeth that you could envision Jimmy Cagney tap dancing to. Some people have dentures that "click" when they talk. I have been royally entertained with a combination "Yankee Doodle" — "Jimmy Cagney Dance" by people who both whistle and click when talking excitedly. Some are so good that I think they ought to be on the stage and charge admission.

Others have dentures that are too loose-fitting. You will also see people who almost lose their dentures when talking animatedly, or even leave them in an ear of corn or apple when they take a hearty bite. People with loose dentures are always adjusting them with their tongue: in and out, sideways, etc. It's rather hard to keep your attention on the conversation when they are doing this.

In my memory, the most vivid example of loose dentures was when I was about 14 years of age. A traveling evangelist was visiting our church for a revival. Mom insisted I go almost every night, and I was glad I did—at the time. This preacher was really going at it with a stormy "hell-fire and damnation" sermon, when all of a sudden — his teeth popped completely out! He must have been a pro at this, because he very deftly caught them about waist high, popped them back into his mouth and didn't miss a beat in his sermon. I was tempted to stand, applaud and yell, "Great catch!" From that moment on, I went to every service expecting to see if he could do it again. His teeth almost came out another 5 or 6 times, but I never got to see if he could make that catch again.

Some ill-fitting dentures rub and irritate the persons mouth. Some of these people, rather than go have a professional do it, will do their own "adjusting": They will take a file or knife and take some off here and there on their denture. I guess that's okay if it helps to make them fit, but I really wish they would do it in private, and not in my presence. It's really distracting to see someone pull out his pocket-knife, open it, take out his dentures and start whittling and scraping on them. I have seen many more men do this than women, because women don't usually carry a pocket knife. I have seen women take a kitchen paring knife and work on their dentures, however.

Irritating dentures also cause another problem. Many people have a tendancy to use their dentures only when they are visiting with guests or eating. At first, it's rather startling when a loved one (even your spouse) leaves their teeth out and you can't recognize them. Their features are completely changed and their speaking voice is in a hard to understand lisp. Sometimes they forget they have them out and greet people at the front door with no teeth. People are startled and look around to see if they have the wrong address.

My grandma (God bless her soul) used to love to come and visit us, and would stay a week or two perhaps. We enjoyed her because she was as sweet as they come, but she had two weaknesses that were sort of irritating once in a while. She was always taking her dentures out at times during the day, and would never wear them in bed at night. We had no problem with that, except she would leave them in the oddest places and never remember where she left them. So when it came time to eat or go someplace we had quite a problem. We would have to search all over to find her teeth. Sometimes, it would be a simple search and we found them quickly, but other times we had quite a search before we found them — generally in some of the strangest places. In spite of all this, we loved her and missed her when she died, but we still have fond memories and laugh about her idiosyncracies.

> *"The four B's of middle age: baldness, bridgework, bifocals and bunions."*

> *"Your teeth are like stars," he said,*
> *and pressed her hand so white.*
> *He spoke the truth, for like the stars,*
> *her teeth came out at night.*

EYES: We don't know why God selected the arbitrary age of 40 to have your eyesight start failing, but that's generally the way it is. This is the magic age — if you haven't had eye trouble before, it's pretty sure to be bifocal time close to the age of 40. Many put off getting glasses as long as possible, but you can always spot and test them easily. Just casually hand them a menu, newspaper, or other items to read, and say, "Would you look at this .....!"" They will always adjust it back and forth to get it in focus if they need glasses. They generally start squinting or opening their eyelids farther as they do this — another giveaway.

Vanity is a factor in putting off getting glasses, or wearing them rarely when you do have them. It makes some sort of crazy sense when you stop to think about it. Very few can know you are getting older and as a result having health problems, but those glasses are a sign right out in front, and everybody will know you are going downhill. That results in the tendency to delay getting glasses until it's obvious that you don't have long enough arms to read anything — no matter the size of the type.

Generally, older persons tend to be "farsighted" — seeing things better at a distance. As said before, when your arms are too short, and someone has to hold it for you or read it to you—the bifocals can no longer be put off. Finally, when you realize your eyes are not going to get any better, you get bifocals. "Breaking in" bifocals is an experience, and not overly pleasant. I don't mean the glasses themselves need to be broken in, I am talking about you getting used to them. For a while you might resemble a blind man who has lost his seeing-eye dog by stumbling into things. You will walk down the stairs with your head held high, not because you're proud of yourself — you are trying to get accustomed to your new glasses.

Many people first getting glasses are vain at this point, too, using the "fast shuffle". For instance they will slip them on quickly to read the menu, and then off and away when they have decided what to order. They problem is, not only are their eyes weak — so's there memory. They forget when it comes time to order and have to whip out those bifocals again. Sometimes you will see their "fast shuffle" 3 or 4 times. Supposedly they believe if they do it fast enough, no one will notice they have to wear glasses.

Sometimes vanity can be risky in ordering in a restaurant. People have been know to order sweet and sour pigs feet with tongue — unintentionally.

Again, because of vanity, many will go to contact lenses. The problem with contact lenses, aside from red, irritated eyes, is losing one or both. Many times you will see people, sometimes in groups, crawling on the floor or ground looking and feeling for contact lenses.

The bottom line is this: Forget your vanity and adjust your priorities. You will find it is a lot easier to get along without sex than it is to do without glasses.

> *"God grant me the Senility to forget the people I never*
> *liked anyway, the good fortune to run into the ones I do,*
> *and the eyesight to tell the difference."*

> *"My face in the mirror isn't wrinkled or drawn.*
> *My house isn't dirty. the cobwebs are gone.*
> *My garden looks lovely and so does my lawn.*
> *I think I might never put my glasses back on."*

HEARING: Hearing loss is a common problem, brought about by one's occupation, or by the simple and natural result of aging. Again, vanity plays a part, letting it get in the way of correcting the problem. It's like the glasses — they feel it's a sign right in front that you've had it, and you are on the downhill side.

Many, with rather severe loss, refuse to be caught wearing a hearing aid, or if they do have one, refuse to turn it on. They act as if they can hear perfectly well. They don't seem to realize that the reason they can hear at all is because others realize their problem and tend to shout about 12 inches from their eardrum. Many will shout back, assuming you are deaf too. Some people seem to be smiling all the time when you talk to them — generally because they can't hear a word you are saying.

Many others, with not quite as severe a hearing loss, still refuse to get and wear a hearing aid. They combine a bit of lip reading with making the person talking repeat things. Another tool they have is a spouse who can hear close by to act as an interpreter, to shout everything close to his or her eardrum. They delude themselves into believing they can hear well — for their age.

Hearing aids are not without their small problems. One is the high frequency squeal they sometimes give off. It's rather interesting in a small church to hear one give that squeal and see one-fourth of the congregation trying to adjust their hearing aid.

Poor Hearing

A man goes to the doctor and complains that his wife can't hear him.

"How bad is it?" the doctor asks.

"I have no idea," says the husband.

"Well, please test her. Stand 20 feet away from her and say something. If she doesn't hear you, get closer and say the same thing. Keep moving closer and repeating the comment until she does hear you. That way we'll have an idea of her range of hearing loss."

So the man goes home and sees his wife in the kitchen chopping up vegetables for dinner.

From 20 feet: "What are we having for dinner?" No answer.

From 10 feet, same thing.

From 5 feet, same thing.

Finally he's standing right behind her ... "What's for dinner?"

She turns around, looks at him and yells "For the FOURTH time ... BEEF STEW!!!"

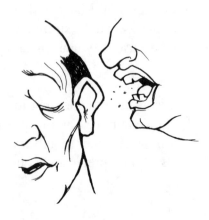

"ORGAN" RECITALS

Mirror, Mirror on the wall,
Who has the biggest hemorrhoids of all?

We have medical problems at every age, and have to take medication or even have operations, but at age 40 you should start having complete medical exams. It seems to get to the point, after 40, that you have too much room in your house and not enough room in your medicine cabinet. Take an inventory of your medicine cabinet. It is pretty sure to contain some or all of the following,: Grecian Formula, Polident, ExLax, Milk of Magnesia, Maalox, Prozac, Depends, blood pressure kit, extra hearing aid batteries, and maybe even Viagara.

It seems to get to the point that most of the names in your "little black book" end with M.D. The "magical" age of 40 seems to bring about some natural but unwelcome medical aspects of the aging process, such as minor aches and pains, seizures, growths, hemorrhoids, intestinal problems, and in some cases, prostate problems. As has been said, "Growing old isn't for sissies."

An examination for prostate should be a regular part of a complete medical examination. Most are reluctant because prostate is found by an exploration where the doctor is intensely interested in a region of your body that you don't even let your wife scrutinize. Basically, for those who have not undergone this degradation, you bend over a table and allow yourself be completely humiliated. (Of course, I don't suppose the doctor is having a great time, either.) People just don't get this scrutiny often enough, because they had almost rather have the problem than the examination.

It is not recommended that you use "How are you?" as part of your greeting with older folks. They are very likely to go into an "organ recital" and tell you all their medical problems. This is generally in a loud voice, so that people can hear from a good distance around. If you are smart, by the time they start this, start edging away to disassociate yourself from him/her.

For instance, the reply to "How are you?" might be: "Oh, I'm not well at all. You know I had major gallstone surgery last Fall. Well, I never have recovered from it. And ...." or "I've got these painful hemorrhoids and can't even sit without my tube. I haven't slept ...." If you are polite enough to listen, they generally go into the most intimate details about their medical troubles, on and on until your eye start glazing over, and you frantically start looking around for escape routes. All this, and all you really wanted to hear in response was, "I'm fine, how are you?"

Many older people seem to get together in the most public places, restaurants, etc., and really get into the most intimate medical problems and bodily functions (pooping) in a sort of "round table" discussion. They enjoy hearing about other's operations and intimate medical problems, so they can "one-up" them. They have the mind-set that the only ones having "minor" operations are others. One of the favorite pastimes or contests is to outdo others on backache stories and operations.

They are generally inclined to give their "organ recital" in a loud voice. They seem to think every one in the restaurant will be fascinated by their most intimate medical problems and body functions, such as painful hemorrhoids, the huge cyst that burst, pooping, etc. They are oblivious to people hurriedly leaving without completing their meals.

I MISS MY MIND

Mirror, Mirror on the wall,
Where did I leave my mind? — I can't recall!

*"My mind works like lightning....one brilliant flash and
then it's gone again."*

*"Don't let your mind go wandering, its too small to go
out by itself."*

*"If a cluttered desk is a sign of a cluttered mind, just
what does an empty desk mean?"*

The mind is a very complex organ, and will you give you problems in
all phases of life. It doesn't seem to do anything but get worse as you
age. It makes commitments that your aging body can't keep, for
instance. The mind and body are often in disagreement. It seems that
when you finally get your mind together — your body starts falling
apart. After this happens, you wonder how you could possibly be over
the hill when you have no recollection of being on top of it.

When old, your mind really plays tricks on you. It is not as resolute,
and you can't even get around to procrastinating. Your mind has always
wandered some, and you went into a little "dream-world" but now it
takes mini-vacations. You might even have been absent-minded before,
but you can't remember whether you were or not. There is no question
in your mind that there is no question in your mind.

A lot of things connected with aging you can get used to: dentures,
glasses, hearing aid, etc., but you really miss your mind when it leaves
on those little vacations. There is nothing you can do about it — you
just have to smile, take a philosophical view of these times, and call
them "senior moments."

A good phase of the mind as you grow older is an attitude that
develops which makes you appear more patient and forbearing. If others only knew. The fact of the matter is that you just don't care any-

more. That's all right, whatever it takes to give you the appearance of learned patience. Of course, some minds are like concrete, all mixed up and permanently set.

What a life! The preacher came to visit me the other day. He said, at my age, I should be thinking about "the hereafter."

I told him, "Oh, I do, all the time! No matter where I am ... in the parlor, upstairs, in the kitchen or down in the basement ... I ask myself, "NOW, WHAT AM I HERE AFTER?"

Gifts for Mom

Three sons left home, went out on their own and prospered. Getting back together, they discussed the gifts they were able to give their elderly mother.

The first said: "I built a big house for our mother."

The second said: "I sent her a Mercedes with a driver."

The third said: "You remember how Mom enjoys reading the Bible. Now she can't see very well. So I sent her a remarkable parrot that recites the entire Bible. It took elders in the church 12 years to teach him, he's one of a kind. Mama just has to name the chapter and verse and the parrot recites it."

Soon thereafter, Mom sent out her letters of thanks....

"Milton," she said, "the house you built is so huge. I live only in one room, but I have to clean the whole house."

"Gerald," she said, "I am too old to travel. I stay most of the time at home so I rarely use the Mercedes. And that driver is so rude! He's a pain!"

"And my dearest, Donald," she said, "the chicken was delicious!"

MEMORY

Mirror, Mirror on the wall,
So what — I'm old! I can't remember it all!

*"Memory is like an orgasm. It's a lot better if you don't
have to fake it."*   — Cray Seymore

*"Those who cannot remember the past will spend a lot
of time looking for their cars in mall parking lots."*
                    — Jay Trachman

Memory many times is a fleeting thing — it comes and goes, more-so in the "Golden Years." We are not talking about Alzheimer's disease. We are talking about the natural memory loss that comes with age. You get very good at telling stories — over and over and over to the same people. And you can safely tell gossip and secrets to your friends — they probably will forget them.

It is not unusual to forget your Social Security number and to call your younger son by the older son's name (and vice-versa). It gets critical when you find yourself in front of an open fridge — wondering why you are there. Even worse is when you pause half-way up the stairs, and suddenly wonder if you were going up or down and why.

At our age we have to change the lyrics of that old song to: "Let me call you sweet-heart — I can't remember your name." It leads to very embarrassing situations. You might be trying to recall someone's name at a party to introduce them, and for the life of you just can't come up with it. You know he is your son, but what was that name?

God is wonderful and wise. He made women so they probably wouldn't bear any children after fifty. He knew they would probably lay that kid down and forget where they left it.

Men, like women, will first forget names, then faces, but they have a further embarrassing deteriorating memory problem: they first forget to pull their zipper up and go around semi-exposed, but the later stage is worse — they forget to pull their zipper down, which is really embarrassing.

Keys must be mentioned when talking about memory. Isn't it an aggravation when you can't remember where you put the keys? Or even worse — you can remember where you put them, but not what they unlock?

Personally, I am proud that I have always had a very good memory. I really have a good mental filing system for copious facts. I do have a little difficulty finding the right file drawer, but still, the facts are in there somewhere. And, I am sure that everything I can't find is in a secure place. Right now, I only have trouble remembering three things: names, faces, and .... hmm .... what was the third thing?

> An elderly couple were experiencing declining memories, so they decided to take a power memory class, where they teach one to remember things by association. Later, the man was talking to a neighbor about how much the class helped him.
>
> "Who was the Instructor?" the neighbor asked.
>
> "Oh, let's see," pondered the man. "Umm...what's that flower, you know, the one that smells real nice but has those thorns...?"
>
> "A rose?" offered the neighbor.
>
> "Right," said the man. He then turned toward his house and shouted, "HEY, ROSE, what's the name of the guy we took that memory class from?"
>
> Two very elderly ladies were enjoying the sunshine on a park bench in Miami. They had been meeting in that park every sunny day for over 12 years, chatting and enjoying each others' friendship. One day, the younger of the two ladies turned to the other and said, "Please don't be angry with me, dear, but I'm embarrassed. After all these years, what is your name? I'm trying to remember, but I just can't."
>
> The older friend stared at her, looking very distressed. She said nothing for two full minutes, and finally with tearful eyes, said, "How soon do you have to know?"

"Who Wrote Whom"

"Just a line to say I'm living,
that I'm not among the dead.
Though I'm getting more forgetful
and mixed up in the head.

I got used to my arthritis,
to my dentures I'm resigned.
I can manage my bifocals,
but I sure do miss my mind.

For sometimes I can't remember
when I stand at the foot of
the stairs,
If I must go up for something,
or I have just come down from there.

And before the fridge so often,
my poor mind is filled with doubt,
Have I just put food away, or
have I come to take some out.

And there's time when it is dark
with my nightcap on my head,
I don't know if I'm retiring, or
just getting out of bed.

So, if it's my turn to write you,
there's no need for getting sore,
I may think that I have written,
and don't want to be a bore.

So, remember that I love you,
and wish you were near.
But now it's nearly mail time
so must say good-bye, dear
There I stand before the mailbox
with a face very red.
Instead of mailing you my letter,
I had opened it instead."

"By the time you're eighty years old you've learned
everything. You only have to remember it."
        — George Burns

A guy was invited to some old friends' home for dinner. His
buddy preceded every request to his wife by endearing
terms, calling her Honey, My Love, Darling, Sweetheart,
Pumpkin, etc. He was impressed since the couple had been
married for sixty years.   While the wife was off in the
kitchen he said to his buddy, "I think it's wonderful that after
all the years you've been married, you still call your wife
those pet names." His buddy hung his head. "To tell you the
truth, I forgot her name about ten years ago."

BOOK II

"FIELD-GUIDE" FOR OLD GEEZER/GEEZERETTES

[There is a special breed of old people. They are known by various names: Old Geezer, Codger, Fogy — even Old Fart. I will use the term Geezer in this book, with the feminine version being Geezerette. I really preferred Old Fart, but somehow it loses something and doesn't sound right to say Fartette.

This special breed of oldsters have a distinctive style of dress, mannerisms and idiosyncrasies. This book is an instructive "how to" on the traits and dress you have to adopt if you aspire to join this select group of Old Geezer/Geezerettes. Even if you don't aspire to be in this group, the following will be a field guide to enable you to recognize and identify them on sight. (By the way, keep it mind — this is all in fun.)]

FASHION FOR OLD GEEZERS

HATS: Wear a brightly colored hat at all times, in all seasons and climates. It is mandatory that you wear a very large hat if you are in the swimming pool. This is the style with old people, and it gives you the excuse not to submerge your head, thereby floating your hairpiece off.

SHIRTS: A good look in casual summer wear is the Mexican style shirt (not tucked in.) If you wish to "get wild," wear a highly and brightly decorated Hilo Hattie shirt (not tucked in). This can be worn at any time but is especially nice on vacation — with a camera slung around your neck to complete the effect.

Always button your shirt up as high as possible, no matter what the season. If you are "robust," and buttoning the top button makes you start to turn blue and feel light-headed, you have a variance to leave it unbuttoned. It is commonly acceptable to leave two or three of the middle buttons undone.

Always wear a sleeveless undershirt that will reveal your hairy armpits. It is acceptable to wear the undershirt without a top shirt in more casual events around home, or to make a short shopping trip to the grocery store, etc.

OUTFITS FOR:

COOLER WEATHER: A comfortable polyester leisure suit is still the favorite — good for all occasions. They come in a variety of nice colors, but lime green is still one of the choice colors. Always wear a white belt with any color. A word of warning: One should be cautious if he is a smoker and wearing polyester — one hot ash on you suit and you could go up in smoke.

Brightly colored jump suits in a lighter fabric are another favorite. These are unbelted or self belted, so the standard white belt is not worn, but white or wing-tipped shoes are still desirable. For a more casual look, wear athletic shoes.

SUMMER/CASUAL: Long Bermuda shorts, sheer Mexican shirt, armpit-revealing under-shirt, white belt, long black over-the-calf stretch hose, and white or wing-tipped shoes make for a snappy summer ensemble. You can also look sharp with socks the same color as your shorts. Remember, button that top button.

A more casual look is attained by substituting a Hilo Hattie shirt for the Mexican, and sandals for footwear with long black or white tube socks. Another popular casual look is attained by wearing long Bermuda shorts, a tank-top or T-shirt, long black or white tube socks, and athletic shoes.

The tank top or T-shirt is especially striking if you have a belly that looks like that of a women pregnant with twins, on the verge of giving birth. In this case, it is a must that you have a design on the shirt showing Bud or Coors.

ACTIVE/ATHLETIC LOOK: For almost all occasions, the warm-up suit is the in thing. They come in a wild variety of patterns and colors. It is, of course, neat to have matching outfits for you and your wife. It looks like a "team effort." Of course, you always wear athletic shoes, and if so inclined, wrist and head sweat bands.

Always carry tennis rackets in your car to impress people with your vim and vigor. It isn't necessary that you actually play tennis (too strenuous). For instance, if you have guests waiting at your house, get your sweat-bands soaking wet, splash some water on your face to look like sweat droplets, put your tennis racket under your arm, and walk into your house, saying to them, "Sorry I'm late — had a close game and just lost track of time."

(Walking, jogging and golf wear covered in later sections.)

POOL/BEACH-WEAR: Always wear sensible wildly patterned and colored boxer style trunks. Do Not wear one of those skimpy Speedos that are about the size of a band-aid. It is pathetic to see an old, pasty, flabby man who has delusions of youthfulness. If you insist on wearing one, have the decency to cover up your groin area with a long T-shirt, cutting down the exposure.

It is acceptable to wear long tube socks with your swim-wear. It's best to remove them before actually getting into the water — they really look sloppy when soaking wet.

NOTE: A vital accessory with any of the outfits discussed above is the clip-on sunglasses — a must. Keep them raised for a neat look, even out in the sun.

SPECIAL NOTE: On trying on any pants or jump suits, always stand out in the sales room and feel of your crotch to see how they fit. If possible, buy pants that can be pulled up under your armpits — another fashion statement.

HAIR-STYLE FOR OLD GEEZERS

If you still have a head of hair and dye it, be sure and select the dark-est brown or black color available. If you are bald or balding, don't bother to spend very much on a hairpiece. Sometimes you can find a real good sale on them. Any will do — after all, a hairpiece is a hair-piece. Again, select the darkest brown or black you can find. It is the "in" thing, even though your face is a mass of wrinkles. It will keep people's attention on something other than those wrinkles.

FASHION FOR GEEZERETTES

EVERY DAY, ALL SEASONS: A very commonly accepted mode of dress is a large unbelted dress. This dress is suitable for all occasions: church, weddings, shopping, funerals, etc. You do not have to have a variety of colors — just pick your favorite color and go with it. This is a one style fits all dress. It really saves you closet space, because you need only two serviceable dresses, one to wear and one to wash.

WARM WEATHER CASUAL: For the casual warm-weather look, Bermuda shorts or jeans are in. These are especially becoming when worn tight enough to enhance your buttocks and create a "wedgie" — definitely eye-catching!

CASUAL ATHLETIC: The rage now is in "casual athletic": the bright, highly patterned and colored warm-up suit, worn with Nikes or some other athletic shoe. Again, a good accessory is a highly visible tennis racket and perhaps wrist and head sweat-bands. All this com-pletes the picture of "I've just had a vigorous workout" look. This out-fit is great for grocery shopping and other errands around town.

POOL/BEACH-WEAR: Science is wonderful. Today there is Lycra, used in making stretch material for swim-wear. It comes in a number of wild colors and patterns. It does stretch and give you a "skin-tight" fit. It is really the style now — so pooh on those old fashioned two-piece affairs with shorts or blouse type bottom and halter top. Forget the extra pounds and the cellulite — you look great!

OTHER ACCESSORIES: For all the outfits above: Snap-on sunglasses are a must for the ladies, too. For more formal events, a huge, shiny vinyl purse, slung on the arm, is chic — especially with matching shoes. For other more casual wear the belted waist bag is the rage.

HAIR/COSMETIC-STYLE FOR GEEZERETTES

HAIR STYLE: If you dye your hair or wear a wig you should select the darkest color, the same as men. Another color with continued popularity is blond — a very natural color for Geezerettes. It sets off the wrinkles nicely, and fools others into thinking you're still having "more fun." Possibly the most natural, yet bold and pleasing look is red. We are not talking about the common red. Imagine, if you will, a carrot that might be lighted from within, looking radioactive. This is the "in" color and style.

COSMETICS: Tammy Faye Baker is a great example to model your makeup after. Like Tammy, layers of mascara is a must.

Lipstick is another important facet of good makeup. Very bright lipstick, heavily and unevenly applied by someone who appears to have palsy is the vogue. The brighter, heavier and more uneven it is applied, the better.

GEEZER/GEEZERETTE
ACTIVITIES/ACTIONS

DRIVING

This must be prefaced by stating that by the time they classify as old Geezer/Geezerettes many have moved to a gated community, and have acquired a large Cadillac, Lincoln or Ford Crown Victoria.

THE CAR: The first essential is having the right type of car. Stay away from small cars — the bigger the better. Drive the biggest one you can find, even if the hood does look as big as a tennis court.

THE POSITION IN THE CAR: Clutch the steering wheel in a tight grip, so that to loosen your hands would require a pry-bar or surgery. No problem if you are small of stature, you can look through the steering wheel. That's sort of fun, because others have to look twice or three times before determining the car actually has a driver. Stare straight ahead, things like pedestrians, on-coming cars, etc. are not your responsibility.

PARKING: If you are lucky enough to find two parking spaces together — take them both! After all, you have a big car. You might even angle across them. It makes it easier to back out when you leave. If you can't find convenient parking, go for the handicapped ones near the building. After all, you are old, and have been through hemorrhoids and/or menopause, haven't you? All that should certainly qualify you for handicapped parking!

GENERAL DRIVING: If you are backing out of your drive into the street, remember that things to the side are not your responsibility, so it doesn't matter if you look up and down the street. People can see you are old and it is their responsibility to avoid you, and their fault if they hit you.

Maintain a good safe speed, say 15 to 20 MPH. Always ride your brakes, or at least tap them often to keep your speed under control.

For highway driving, you can really "put the pedal to the metal" and get your speed up as high as 45 MPH. Again don't bother to signal lane changes. You can change lanes at any time — others coming from behind should be watching and avoiding you.

On city streets there are many potential hazards—trees, street lights, sidewalks, etc. Slow down or stop abruptly for each one. At the 4-way stop signs, act as if you are going to stop — then plunge right ahead and go through. Other drivers need to "stay on their toes."

It's the same on city streets as it is on the highway: you can change lanes at any time without a signal, as other drivers have the responsibility to be alert. If you plan to make a turn, begin to signal at least four blocks ahead. You can, if you want, travel down the turning lane well before you actually get to your exit. If you signal wrong on a turn, — no problem! You are old and people will understand.

You can pull out onto the freeway at your convenience in front of other drivers — they are alert and will not hit you. You can be assured of that when you hear their brakes screech and see them swerve in your rearview mirror.

These are the basic suggestions for good Geezer/Geezerette driving. On occasion there will be drivers passing you on Interstate or city streets, honking and yelling something you can't hear, and making some sort of hand signal. They are probably yelling and signaling: "Good job! You are a number one driver!" When this happens — be proud!

NOTE: Most Old Geezer/Geezerettes do not use turn signals. If you happen to see one with his signal blinking — ignore it. It was probably either turned on accidentally at home when he got in the car, or was on when he purchased the car.

"ON THE ROAD AGAIN": It's a great life! Get yourself a Winnebago and stock it up to spend a lot of time on the road. Before you even think about starting you need some bumper stickers like "Spending My Kids Inheritance." A great one is "If You See This R.V. Rockin' — Don't Bother Knockin'." That will fool everybody and if nothing else will thoroughly embarrass your kids.

You must stock up before each trip with the essentials: Grecian Formula, Polident, ExLax, Milk of Magnesia, Maalox, Prozac, Depends, blood pressure kit, extra hearing aid batteries, high fiber cereal, and other food. Be sure you have your complete Geezer/Geezerette wardrobe along, suitable for all occasions. Make a list of all these items and have an "essential check" before you leave on any trip.

Your driving can be much the same as driving a car. These Winnebagos can take it so you can get her up to 45 MPH and keep her there. You will need a CB radio to call your "good buddies" and check on the "County Mounties." After all, they might ticket you if they catch you going at the reckless speed of 45 MPH.

Parking and setting up for the night is no problem. There are plenty of good mall and store parking lots along your route. Why pay those R.V. Park fees? Avoid truck-stops — those semi drivers leave their rigs running all night, and those diesels are noisy — enough to even drown out the sound of your generator running. When you reach the warm climes, you might decide to spend more than one night in the parking lot. You might even get your chairs out and soak up some rays. It really makes for an economical trip.

> *As a senior citizen was driving down the freeway, his car phone rang.*
>
> *Answering, he heard his wife's voice urgently warning him, "Herman, I just heard on the news that there's a car going the wrong way on Interstate 280. Please be careful!"*
>
> *Herman said, "It's not just one car. There's hundreds of them!"*

> *(Four old Geezers having coffee and talking in a café.)*
> *"My arm is so weak I can hardly hold this coffee cup."*
> *"Yes, I know, my cataracts are so bad I can't see to pour the coffee."*
> *"I can't turn my head because of the arthritis in my neck."*
> *"My blood pressure pills make me dizzy."*

"I guess that's the price we pay for getting old."
"Well, it's not all bad. We should be thankful that we can still drive!"

Out For A Drive

Two elderly women were out driving in a large car, both could barely see over the dashboard. As they were cruising along they came to an intersection. The stoplight was red but they just went on through. The woman in the passenger seat thought to herself, "I must be losing my mind, I swear we just went through a red light."

After a few more minutes they came to another intersection and the light was red again, and again they went right through. This time the woman in the passenger seat was almost sure that the light had been red, but was really concerned that she was mistaken. She was getting nervous and decided to pay very close attention to the road and the next intersection to see what was going on.

At the next intersection, sure enough, the light was definitely red and they went right through. She turned to the woman driving and said, "Mildred! Did you know we just ran through three red lights in a row! You could have killed us!"

Mildred turned to her and said, "Oh, am I driving?"

SPORTS?

"JOGGING"/WALKING — SPORTS?

JOGGING/WALKING: Jogging is not recommended for the geriatric set. If you insist on jogging — go well equipped with hospitalization insurance that has a good orthopedic rider, "911" pager, Medic Alert bracelet, nitroglycerin pills, and water bottle. It also wouldn't hurt to have a shirt with your identification, home address and even your personal physician printed on it. You never know.

A special note about this and other active exercises — it does activate your kidneys and bladder, and other body functions. So, unless you happen to be wearing Depends, make sure there are numerous rest stops along the way. You will need them. If you don't have something handy, you might succumb to "bladder panic" or "other panic" and do something that could get you arrested.

Walking is good exercise. The outfit recommended for jogging and walking is running shorts and/or sweats, both brightly colored. With that you wear athletic running shoes and neon colored wrist and head sweat-bands. A Sony Walkman with headphones is a must.

The jogging/walking form is the distinctive thing a Geezer/Geezerette must know. Both are about the same and at about the same speed. Keep the arms and legs stiff and you lean forward as if you are facing a gale wind. Then do a short of shuffle-step forward. At the same time work your arms violently and spasmodically — like you are having a problem with the central nervous system or brain. You are apt to cause some excitement if you jog/walk near traffic. Distracted drivers often either call 911 to summon medical help or laugh so hard they lose control and hit trees or have head-on collisions — not a good thing!.

TENNIS: Tennis is a good sport if you play with one of your approximate age and ability. This would naturally reduce the action to the appearance of slow motion, and be good exercise and helpful for both. This slow-motion tennis could not be classed as a spectator sport, however. Any one watching would probably soon doze off, and fall off their chair or bleacher seat.

The benefit from this slow-motion tennis would not be much in the physical gain, but it would enable the Geezer/Geezerette to walk around in his/her snappy tennis togs, racket in hand, and really impress people with their vigor.

GOLF: Golf is a good Geezer/Geezerette sport. You can claim it's good for your health and act like you walk all eighteen holes, carrying your own clubs. Don't mention the cushy golf carts you ride around in getting as close as possible, to keep the walking to a bare minimum. Let people think you are on a real exercise kick.

The out fit for the Old Geezerette is simple and practical, with a bright golf skirt, a simple top and shoes, and a brightly colored sun-visor. The Old Geezer should let his imagination run wild when selecting his golfing outfit. The pants should be so bright and garish—they were surely made by a blind man in a room with no light. He should choose with care the same wild colors in shoes, shirt and cap. It all goes together to make a striking outfit.

NOTE: The "sport" of choice with many Geezer/Geezerettes is the game of Bingo. They think that handling six cards at one time is exercise enough.

> *"As a person gets older, bingo becomes more and more fascinating."*

MAKE THEM HEAR YOU!

Let's say you have had some hearing loss. Always assume that others are hard of hearing just like you. Shout all your conversations no matter where you are or no matter what those conversations are about. That way, you can share with everyone within a 50 yard radius news about your spouse leaving you, grandchildren into drugs, intimate medical problems, your bodily functions, your medications, etc. This shouted narrative is especially well received in a nice restaurant, a movie theater or at a party. Keep this in mind, you have to make them hear you so they won't miss any important points.

"ORGAN RECITALS"
(A MUST FOR THE GEEZER/GEEZERETTE)

Everyone is intensely interested in hearing about your operations, sick-nesses, medications — even your most intimate medical problems, such as painful hemorrhoids. They are also interested in your bodily functions, such as "pooping." Take every opportunity to fill them in. If someone, friend or stranger, says to you, "Hey, how you doing?", that

is your opportunity to give them both barrels — the full load. After all, they asked because they wanted to know, didn't they?

One tip: Always let the other person go first with his medical problems and listen carefully. That way you can always embellish your "organ recital" so it will top theirs and really impress them.

Carry pictures! They say a picture is worth a thousand words. Carry pictures, along with those of your grandchildren, of your angioplasty or other operations — no matter how intimate. Everyone will be fascinated by them just as they will be by the pictures of your grandchildren. It will show them you have had the most serious operations and the most extraordinary grandchildren.

Restaurants, parties, etc. are excellent places to give your organ recital. Along with your other problems, you probably have some hearing loss, and assume others are also hearing impaired. So in a nice restaurant be sure to give your organ recital in a loud clear voice.

Start with pooping — telling about what fiber you eat and what medicine you prefer to take to help you poop. Since it is in the same area of your body, work from pooping into your painful hemorrhoids. Work through your operations showing pictures and naming medications for various things. A good one to end with is the baseball-size cyst—how it burst and the stuff that looked like puss came out. It is guaranteed, at this point, that the people at all adjoining tables will have stopped eating, no doubt intrigued by your narrative. Some seem to have left rather abruptly — perhaps because of an emergency.

> *"Remember, old folks are worth a fortune, with silver
> in their hair, gold in their teeth, stones in their kidneys,
> lead in their feet, and gas in their stomachs."*

> *"Be nice to your children because they will choose your
> rest home."*
>
> — Phyllis Diller

FINALLY —
THEGEEZER/GEEZERETTE
ATTITUDE

The true Geezer/Geezerette must have a certain attitude. Your attitude as an old Geezer/Geezerette, includes such things as dressing in clothes of your own style, driving pretty much as you see fit, giving organ recitals at every opportunity in the most public places and laying guilt trips on your children/grandchildren.

Attitude toward children/grandchildren for instance: When you talk or write to your children or grandchildren, always lay a guilt trip on them about not coming to see you. Talking to them in a slightly whimpering martyrs voice will work wonders. Something like "I know you are too busy to come and see me, but that's all right — I'll be okay."

Another plan is to pit your children against each other. For instance: when talking to Susan, mention the nice letter you received from Jim and how very thoughtful and attentive he is. The implication is loud and clear. And when they do visit, spend most of the time complaining how lonely you are and how that they never come to see you.

If your attitude has been refined as suggested up to this point, you are ready to go to the highest stage of attitude — that of a C.O.F. or Crusty Old Fart (male or female). As the name implies you are expected to be crotchety about your rights as an old person. Some instances: Demand your rightful senior discount at any time and any place. Glare at the people in a line until someone offers to let you in front of them. Always expect others to get up and give you the most comfortable seat. If necessary, single someone out and glare at them till they relent. Always demand all of your senior "rights".

People expect you to be crotchety, eccentric and weird — don't disappoint them When you become known as a Crusty (or Crotchety) Old Fart, you can get by with almost anything.

BOOK III

AGING: PROBLEMS — MYTHS & TRUTHS — SOLUTIONS

[The previous two books were basically "tongue-in cheek" humor, for the purpose of helping those in the aging process to learn to laugh at some of their circumstances and have a more humorous attitude in dealing with problems they may already have or will face.

This third and final book is in a serious vein and has a three-fold purpose, and is divided into three sections. Section I, titled "AGING: THE PROBLEMS," is to identify and discuss some of the circumstances and problems connected to the aging process.

Section II, titled "Aging: IT'S MYTHS & TRUTHS," is a serious discussion of the myths and the dispelling of them with truths about aging. There are so many misconceptions about aging that people look forward to it with dread, and try, by various means, to fight it all the way. It is a futile battle. Aging is very much mandatory — but growing up is optional.

Section III, titled "Aging: THE SOLUTIONS" can be classed as somewhat inspirational, written with the intent to encourage and inspire you to look at your own aging circumstances with the right positive attitude— one which includes resolve, optimism, laughter and humor. I can only hope it will also include a healthy spirituality.

This really is your "Golden Age" if you allow it to be. Let me ask you a question: "Would you rather live out the remainder of you life with quality—positiveness, friends, joy, laughter and actual enjoyment? Or would you rather live out your life with self-pity, loneliness, depression and bitterness?" If you truly would rather not climb out of your rut and opt for the latter, you might as well read no further, and just toss this book into the wastebasket — it might deepen your rut. On the other hand, if you want a quality life, read on and take my humble suggestions to heart. Accept aging! If you truly want a long life, you must be willing to grow old gracefully. I pray that my words help you along the way.]

SECTION I
Aging: THE PROBLEMS

Aging has been a major factor in our lives ever since God created man. Has man gained any more understanding and acceptance of aging through the years? No. In fact, man actually has less understanding and acceptance of this inevitable process. Today man holds many misconceptions and false ideas about this perfectly natural process that were not held in ancient times. It has become traumatic to many individuals to the point of actual dread of growing old.

> *"One of the hardest tricks to master is how to grow old gracefully. We hope for a long life but hate to grow old in order to achieve it."*

"AGE MEASUREMENT": For man, there are three distinct measurements of age. There is, of course, the regular chronological age, measured in years. There is physiological age, measured in the condition of one's body and it's vital functions. Finally, there is psychological age, measured by relationships and one's attitude to others and circumstances.

> *"We do not count a man's years until he has nothing else to count."*
>
> — Ralph Waldo Emerson

PHASES OF LIFE:

The life of children is somewhat happy and carefree, having very few fears or disappointments. This is the start of their formative years, where they start learning moral values as their body develops.

Youth is very busy, experiencing new things and ideas, frustrations and fears, with not too much thought of what the future holds. Later, they have some trepidation about the future. This is still part of their formative years when they get the moral values and personal attributes to determine, to some degree, what sort of person they will be.

The "young adult"(ages 19 - 37) age is the age of choice. In this stage, they choose their spouse, their career or work, and many will choose their church affiliation. They have some apprehensions about making a success of their lives, and attaining a goal or making their mark. They may even make some career changes during this period. They are not overly concerned about aging until the later years.

For many, middle-age (ages 38 - 50) is the first truely traumatic phase of life. Even though they may have achieved much and have considerable authority — they are dissatisfied. Many manage to work their way through this feeling, and settle down to normal lives. Others remain so discontented they go into what is known as "mid-life crisis."

MIDDLE-AGE & MID-LIFE CRISIS: "Old age" does not necessarily start at any particular chronological age, but many indications of aging appear at this time. Aches and pains, minor medical problems, gray hair, wrinkles, sexual problems, etc., happen during this time. When one or more of these signs first appear, they are a shock to the individual and make he/she realize the aging process has started. It is hard to get used to the fact that your once vigorous body is starting to lose ground.

Because of minor medical problems, middle-aged people start worrying about their health, even though they may be perfectly healthy for their age. They may start having vision and hearing loss, and this is bothersome. Sometimes they develop a paunchy belly they can no longer flatten, along with love handles.

At this point women start worrying about female problems that include menopause, sexual gratification, and their fading beauty. Men are concerned about declining sexual performance and their failing prowess. Perhaps the most singular vexatious thing with some is misgivings about their sexual performance. Both men and women regret aspirations and goals not met — feeling that their lives could have been richer, fuller and even more successful. All of these factors are intensified by the nagging feeling that this is the middle of their life and it is half gone. All of this brings about mid-life crisis in some.

People react differently to this mid-life crisis. Some will grow up mentally and work their way through to rich, full and satisfying lives. Others, however will "get the crazies" and plunge into new relationships, new careers and new interests—without weighing the consequences. They are going for some illusive goal of self-gratification. Unfortunately, they often desert a lovely and loving family in their quest.

> *"One of the chief pleasures of middle age is looking back at all the people you didn't marry."*

"DENIAL": It is at this stage of life, to a degree influenced by narcissism or vanity, denial of growing old is initiated. This denial is evidenced by endeavors to hide aging by dressing and acting young, and using cosmetics and plastic surgery to appear younger.

Women are the primary users of "miracle" creams and cosmetic surgery (body, breast and facial) to preserve the appearance of remaining young, but it has become increasingly prevalent with men. Both women and men, in growing numbers, are using cosmetic surgery.

To be very blunt, this rejection of the inevitability of growing old is foolish — as foolish as it would be to refuse to abandon childhood.

It is reminiscent of the play "Peter Pan" where Peter pranced and flew around, always stating emphatically that he would "never grow up."

> *"I must be getting absent-minded. Whenever I complain that things aren't what they used to be, I always forget to include myself."*
>
> — George Burns

RETIREMENT: Retirement is sometimes a stressful period in life. Full enjoyment of retirement is a matter of attitude — whether it is looked at negatively or positively. With the right positive attitude, it is a goal that can be looked forward to with great anticipation.

Some have a negative attitude and insist on working until they are forced to retire — then resent it. They will sometimes hang on until their abilities and interest have waned. At this time they have possibly become an aggravation to associates and/or co-workers or employees — and will eventually become more and more unpopular.

If your main interest is centered in a certain job, trade or business, retirement can be a traumatic shock. This can spawn many unwarranted fears such as living with reduced income, loneliness, being useless, etc. — just to name some.

> *"The only difference between a rut and a grave is the depth."*

BAD ATTITUDES ON AGING

Many have developed bad attitudes toward the inevitability of growing old. There is a growing discontent rather than acceptance of this certainty. You may have some of these bad attitudes even though you are otherwise intelligent, competent and qualified. These attitudes are many times evidenced by being negative and sarcastic, complaining, casting blame, having self-pity, not laughing as much, etc. This will make your home a battle arena, with a minor battle area everywhere you go. To be very blunt, your bad attitudes will take its toll on you, your family and others with whom you have any relationships or contact.

Let's identify and discuss some of these bad attitudes:

FIGHTING THE INEVITABLE: There is a great energy waste going on. No, it isn't gas, solar or any other such thing. It is the extreme waste of energy in fighting the inevitability of aging. This frame of mind will be conductive to many of the following attitudes:

NEGATIVISM: This is the feeling as stated by Murphy's Law that "everything that can go wrong — probably will." People with this perspective feel that any of the natural events and circumstances of aging are part of a bad hand dealt to them.

IRRITATION: One of the things we don't need because of the waste of energy and the changing of our focus in aging is to let common irritations bother us. These come through events and the actions or inactions of others. Examples are delays in traffic, doctor's office, airports, and the cost of everything from peanuts to cars. There are numerous pet irritations including anything as inconsequential as the weather, who won or lost a game or the unintentional words of others.

BLAME: This attitude is one in which a person tries to find a scapegoat for circumstances or events, even those that are the natural result of aging. You will go to the point of blaming others, yourself, or God.

If you blame others, this puts an ever-widening chasm between yourself and them. This will eventually ruin any relationships by alienating others — making for a far less than desirable situation.

If you blame yourself, you are clinging to the past and further lowering your self-esteem. Self-blame and self-guilt are always onerous loads to take on.

The worst sort of blame is that of blaming God. With spirituality, God is the source of the power we need to face with courage life's aging circumstances and occurrences. God does not want us to be unhappy, and will help us if we ask.

GUILT/REGRET: This attitude says: "I blew any chances I had. If I had it to do over, I sure would do things differently" — (with family, friends, finances, job, etc.) Regret or guilt of things in the past are a heavy but unnecessary burden to take on. Many are burdened with regrets when a good phase of life is over or at the loss of a relationship — forgetting the privilege of having that person or good phase in their life.

> *"Enjoy the Spring of Love and Youth,*
> *to some good angel leave the rest;*
> *For Time will teach thee soon the truth,*
> *there are no birds in last year's nest!"*
> — Henry Wadsworth Longfellow

> *"Many people use their youth to make their old age miserable."*

SELF-PITY: This is a deadly trap that many facing the aging clock fall into. It's the attitude that says, "I don't deserve this — I've been dumped on! No one cares whether I am sick or even if I live or die." There are people who end up wallowing in this mud-bath of self pity, picturing themselves almost like victims of a nuclear accident.

This attitude is termed deadly because it is harmful to you and it alienates others who love you. Constant whining will eventually spoil your relationships with others.

USELESSNESS: This is a common feeling, even by a competent, resourceful individual who may have had a significant role in the past. It seems to come out strongly in those who have just retired in the last 3 - 4 years. This feeling seemingly says, "I am over the hill, I have nothing left to contribute. No one would even notice if I weren't here. I wouldn't be missed by many if I were dead."

FEAR: This is a very common attitude among the aging. They have fear for the future. This speaks to concerns about having an adequate income, loss of friends or family members, failing health, failing mind, dependency and death. Everyone has some concern over these things. The problem arises if you have this attitude to the degree that it affects your actions and living.

"I've found a formula for avoiding these exaggerated fears of age: You take care of every day — let the calendar take care of the years."
                                          — Ed Wynn

DEPENDANCY/DEATH FEAR: This attitude was mentioned above, but is discussed separately because of the prominence in people's minds.

Fear of dependancy is simply the fear of becoming helpless, debilitated — and dependant on or perhaps even a burden to your children or relatives. The extreme is the fear of abandonment. This is a very frightening state of mind.

Fear of death is not so much the fear of the moment of death, but of the unknown — the perhaps painful prelude to dying, and to what happens after death. [No one really wants to die — I certainly don't. I am enjoying my "Golden Years." However, being a Christian and believing in life after death I can look at my inevitable death with more serenity of mind.]

"Better to ride
The rising tide
Of time's incessant call
Than to tussle in rage
With advancing age —
And get nowhere at all."

"We hope to grow old, yet we fear old age; that is we are willing to live, and afraid to die."
                                          — Bruyere

SECTION II
Aging: MYTHS & TRUTHS

[Today's society commonly holds many negative miscon-
ceptions and false ideas about aging. With this section I
will list and discuss some of those generally held myths
and try to dispel them with truths. When I say truths I
mean the actualities or evidence gleaned from science,
medicine, etc., eliciting facts which are contrary to these
myths.

I have no illusions that this small book will change
the widely held misconceptions of society. I do have
hope that my words may help some to a better under-
standing and thus enable them to face their aging cir-
cumstances with a positive attitude. If I do, this book will
have been worth the effort. I sincerely hope and pray
that it helps many in this respect.]

MYTH — MEMORY: A goodly amount of memory
loss is inevitable with advanced age. It can even develop
into Alzheimer's.

TRUTH: First, Alzheimer's is a disease that causes memory loss
among other things. It is not the result of memory loss.

It does seem in everyday life, as we grow older, we forget things
more easily. However, the degree of any memory loss is highly exaggerated and is not necessarily a natural result of aging. Look about you,
even the young and young adults have memory lapses. It just doesn't
follow that these same forgetful oldsters can recall events of youngsters
and even recite, with great clarity, poetry, etc. learned when they were
young. Stress, anxiety and illness are common among older people and
can affect memory — but this is memory lapse, not memory loss!
People of all ages have "senior moments" — momentary memory
lapses.

Another factor: You must practice or exercise your brain section
dealing with memory, or it will get sluggish, just like your body will get

lax, weak and lazy without proper exercise. Remember the old saying: "Use it or lose it!"

MYTH — INTELLIGENCE QUOTIENT or I.Q.: Your I.Q. will inevitably decline with age, and you will not be able to logically think as well as previously.

TRUTH: Oldsters will perhaps follow different logical extrapolating or logical sequences in their cognitive processes, but their I.Q. does not decrease. There is no scientific evidence that basic I.Q. does decrease. It may give this appearance if other facets such as illness, etc., affect the thinking processes.

MYTH — RETIREMENT: The compulsory retirement age is arbitrarily set at 65. There is a logical scientific and medical basis for this policy.

TRUTH: There is no logical basis for this policy. One's abilities <u>do not</u> automatically and suddenly diminish at this age. In fact, he/she might be even more productive than in their younger years. The exception to this is retiring from a physically or emotionally strenuous job when one's physical or mental abilities has decreased to a marked degree. This is often caused by illness, accidents or other things not related to one's occupation.

Actually, the retirement age should be variable, according to the individual — like the athlete, who knows when his competence wanes. He will generally opt to retire before his performance discomfits him or even embarrasses him. One generally knows when one's abilities wane to the point his/her productivity drops, and should acknowledge it in time to go on to other things.

MYTH — "USEFULNESS": One's usefulness (productivity and contribution) will decline to the point where he/she will be of little value or use to society, and they will be sort of a drag.

TRUTH: The feeling of uselessness by individuals is all too common. However, one's productivity and contribution dwindles only in direct relation to his/her attitude and motivation. You can very well say that this is a self-inflicted condition. If one has a negative or pessimistic perspective with no motivation left, he/she will probably become a self-pitying introvert with less value to society. The reaction of others to this outlook will probably exacerbate and add the feeling of being unneeded and unwanted.

On the other hand, if one has a the positive attitude and motivation, he/she will be productive and remain valuable to society to any age. They will never have that feeling of uselessness. It is simply up to the individual's choice whether to "shoot him/herself in the foot" or not.

> **MYTH — HEALTH:** Old is like a disease, in that it is synonymous with disability, sickness and ill health.

TRUTH: Vital organs: heart, liver, lungs, etc., will last for a certain maximum time. They will wear out earlier, however, due to neglect and abuse. Old age in itself does not automatically bring disability, sickness and ill health. We tend to exercise less, eat more and neglect care of our bodies — this contributes to many of these afflictions. There are some medical problems that come upon us with age, but are held to a minimum with proper exercise, diet, medical care and regular physical examinations. The various parts of your body will remain relatively healthy with appropriate care. It's your body, and you only have the one — take care of it!

> **MYTH — MIND/BRAIN:** People are intrinsically less vigorous and active mentally with age. Their thinking and reasoning prowess will inevitably diminish as they grow older.

TRUTH: It is widely agreed by experts that oldsters are not losing their mental power, they are just not "using it" often enough. Perhaps it is low self-esteem and negativity toward others and circumstances that are the root of this problem of inaction.

At any age, the brain (or intellect) is kept active and well-functioning by exercising it, and by keeping an active interest in things and new ideas. Exercising your body keeps your muscles toned up, inactivity causes them to be weak and sluggish. Your brain is the same as the rest of your body — it needs exercise to keep it sharp and active. Again, attitude plays the key role — you can control the age of the mind, and keep it energetic and dynamic.

> **MYTH — ENJOYMENT:** The latter years of life are inherently a time of misery — joy and enjoyment cannot be expected.

TRUTH: The above statement could not be farther from the truth. The basics misery or lack of joy and enjoyment is simple: Attitude! You can self-destruct and make yourself absolutely miserable with a negative and pessimistic outlook. With this sort of demeanor you are capable of taking all joy, enjoyment and meaning out of life.

With the right positive attitude, it is a fact that age 60 through 80 can be the most enjoyable and useful time of your life. You can even hold off some incapacity with this positivity and courage.

> **MYTH — SENILITY:** When one reaches a certain number of years, the chances of becoming senile are high — it just goes along with the process of aging.

TRUTH: This is pure hogwash. There are people who, with a very negative and pessimistic attitude, have voluntarily opted to withdraw from society. They have at some age or another put their brain and body on hold and don't utilize or exercise either. They are a product of their own making, withdrawing into their own little world. The exception of course, is illness or disease affecting the brain and body causing this condition. The terms "senile" or "senility" were coined to classify people in this state. There is no reason to dread senility, you are probably on the ball enough to have no qualms about it.

> **MYTH — NEW IDEAS/CHANGE:** "You can't teach an old dog new tricks." This an old saying epitomizing the idea that your ability to learn and absorb new ideas and change diminishes with age.

TRUTH: Your mind has not diminished with age. If your outlook and motivation are positive, you can assimilate new ideas and changes. It simply is not a matter of age, but of attitude.

> *"They can't call you an old dog as long as you are learning new tricks."*

> *"You're never too old to learn— but that's no reason to keep putting it off."*

> **MYTH — ACHIEVEMENT:** Old age is when you are "over the hill" and is a time of decline — you cannot anticipate any achievements or accomplishments that are meaningful.

TRUTH: In fact, the contrary is true. Most seniors have gained a great deal of knowledge and experience. You are much better qualified to achieve than when younger. Your mind, along with this extra knowledge is generally more ordered and resolved in it's thinking processes.

There is a statistic that really says it all: At least 65 percent of the worlds greatest achievements were by people who were over 60 years of age! Blows this myth and your mind, doesn't it? Check it out for yourself — it's a fact!

SECTION III
Aging: THE SOLUTIONS

[At first glance, this title may be somewhat misleading for some, thinking I might be talking about the solution to the whole problem of aging. Note that "solutions" is plural. I am talking about the various problems and circumstances, imagined or real, of aging, and their solutions.

I am classifying this section of the book the "inspirational" section. This is an elementary exposition of what I perceive to be "solutions" to most, if not all, of the problems of aging. I hope to inspire you to face those problems with the right attitude: laughter, humor, resolve and courage. Hopefully, logic and facts will inspire you to rid yourself of imagined problems, thereby making what time you have left in life more pleasant.

On a personal note I truly care for others, and trust that some of my words might inspire you to become a Christian if you are not already one. It is a very simple process of believing. What have you got to lose? In my opinion you have everything to gain when you become a Christian, as well as everything to lose if you do not. A healthy spirituality will do wonders in giving you the mental and physical strength to face all problems — especially those connected with aging.

Believe me when I say, "I care for you.", and want you to be happy. I hope and pray that none of the words in this book offend you, but instead inspire you and others to a richer, fuller and more gratifying life in your latter years.]

"Let me but live my life from year to year,
With forward face and unreluctant soul.
Not hurrying to, nor turning from the goal;

Not mourning for things that disappear
In the dim past, nor holding back in fear
From what the future veils, but wit a whole
And happy heart, that pays its toll
To you and age, and travels on with cheer.
So let the way wind up the hill or down,
O'er rough or smooth, the journey will be joy;
Still seeking what I sought when but a boy,
New friendship, high adventure, and a crown,
I shall grow old, but never lose life's zest,
Because the road's last turn will be the best."
                                   — Henry van Dyke

"Grow old along with me!
The best is yet to be,
The last of life, for which the first was made.
Our times are in his hand."
                                   — Robert Browning

Aging is a largely misunderstood process. People equate aging with growing old. In my opinion they are very different. As I have mentioned previously, we measure age in three ways. *Chronological* age is measured in years, *physiological* (physical) age by the condition of your body and its vital functions; *psychological* (mind) age in how you react to aging circumstances and to others.

The bottom line? *"Aging"* is a biological process that we all go through, *"growing old"* is really a state of mind. There are many people who have been *"old"* in their demeanor all of their adult life, to say the least.

"To keep the heart unwrinkled, to be hopeful, kindly, cheerful, reverent that is to triumph over old age."
                                   — Thomas B. Aldrich

"Age does not depend upon years, but upon temperament and health. — Some men are born old, and some never grow old."
                                   — Tryon Edwards

Incidentally, *"senility"* or *"being senile"* is often equated with *"aging"* and/or *"growing old."* They are not synonymous. You can become *"senile,"* but only as a result of extreme weakness or debility as a result of aging. It is not a natural result, however. Most people do not become senile, in the strictest sense of the word. They become senile by mentally choosing to avoid activity and involvement and by not desiring further growth or relationships. In other words, one can voluntarily become senile, or a close version of it.

We must learn to accept aging with positive philosophical realism. To say that old age does not have it's problems is to be misleading. Naturally it brings unpleasant and unwelcome circumstances. Sometimes those circumstances are greatly misunderstood and exaggerated, and this preys on many minds.

It has been the experience of many that the period from 50 to 80 years of age can be the most enjoyable, gratifying, useful and productive phase of their lives.

The *"growing old"* state of the mind would not happen if one has a positive outlook. Let's forget the negative and discuss some of the positive aspects or solutions to the problem of aging. Let's explore some facets of your body, it's faculties and "life after 50," that should give you a more optimistic outlook on your own aging process.

"As I approve of a youth that has something of the old man in him, so I am no less pleased with an old man that has something of the youth. He that follows this rule, may be old in body, but can never be so in mind."
— Cicero

YOUR PHYSICAL BODY

HEALTH: There is no doubt that most will have health problems as they age. Some will be the natural result of the aging process, but some will be of our own doing. Medical science has advanced greatly. Much can be done with new drugs and medical procedures to stem or eliminate the adverse effects of many diseases or other health problems — so the outlook can be optimistic.

Of course, the body simply wears out at some age, and you can't expect a doctor to "put scrambled eggs back into the shell." The important thing is to have complete periodic medical examinations, so problems can be discovered while they are still fixable. Many neglect this simple procedure until they have dire symptoms.

"From the day of your birth
  Til you ride in a hearse
There's nothing that's happened
  That couldn't have been worse."

"A pessimist is someone who feel bad when he feels good for fear he'll feel worse when he feels better."

OBESITY: When one ages, the usual tendency is to exercise less. If you exercise less, with age your body's metabolism will change and you will require less calories. This, of course, results in gaining more weight with body fat — something you do not need. With increased weight, the inclination is to exercise even less, which stores even more calories, — and so on ....This intensifies the problem of obesity. The problem with all this extra weight is that it can contribute to many medical problems in your body.

Consider most doctors and their orders. For many ailments such as heart problems, blood pressure, diabetes, etc., the doctor will prescribe diet and exercise along with drugs. In most cases, of course, diets are designed to cut down the extra body fat. Exercise is recommended to help use up calories, to reduce stored fat, and to tone up your body. Most of the time this exercise is as simple as walking.

The bottom line is: It's your body, the only one you have, and as there are no real good replacement parts — take care of it!
"The best thing to save for your old age is yourself."

DISABILITY/DEPENDANCE: One of the more common dreads in aging is of becoming debilitated or enfeebled by disease to the point of dependance on others to care for you.

Today, due to great advances in medical science, many diseases can be held in check, if not cured, and thus will not lead to incapacitation.

First and foremost the aging process does not automatically bring on a disease that could possibly debilitate you to the point of dependence. That happens to relatively few. In some cases, however, the medical prognosis is eventual disability. That "puts the ball in your court," when you have to face this condition with grace, courage and positivity.

Do all you can for yourself for as long as humanly possible. It would also be well-advised for your loved ones to take this to heart. They naturally want to do everything for you. They can help you most by allowing you to do everything you possibly can for yourself. You can do more than you can imagine if you have the courage to try.

By all means, do not fall into the fatal trap of self-pity, frustration and bitterness. You can do many things for yourself — by convincing yourself that you can do it. Don't let yourself be turned into a helpless invalid if at all possible.

ABILITIES & FACULTIES

THE MIND: When God created us, He did so in His likeness in that we are thinking, feeling and rational beings. He gave us a brain, an extremely complex mechanism. In fact, it is the most remarkable and complex mechanism known to man. You have heard computers equated with the brain. It is a fact: There is no computer built, nor likely to be invented, that comes close to duplicating the speed and capabilities of the human brain. Even more remarkable, some noted scientists and psychologists have come to the conclusion that man actually uses only one-half of his cerebral ability.

Our basic intelligence (I.Q.) does not increase after our earlier years, but it is not materially reduced with age. The fact is, we make better use of those mental powers. Another fact is that by adding the experience and knowledge we gain along the way can develop into true wisdom in our later years. The mind can keep growing for as long as you live. It can produce new thoughts, new interests, and be stimulated if you allow it to do so.

The most productive output of the mind in our life-span is the latter part. Statistics prove that some 65% of the world's greatest achievements were by people over 60 years of age! It is true that these may be gifted people, but there are gifted people in all age phases, so that amazing average holds true. The message we get from these statistics is that you have the ability, no matter your age, to be productive and attain some achievements of your own. Granted, those achievements may not be in the same class as "the world's greatest" but they are just as important — for you, at least. The old saying "Use it or lose it" is highly applicable to the mind. If you exercise your mind, it will last longer — that is a fact. Keep an open and active mind — the more you use your brain, the more brain you will have to use. If you let your mind get indolent and lethargic, it has an adverse effect on you and everything about you.

Before we leave the subject of the mind, we need to discuss a common fallacy about it. This fallacy or myth is that people, when reaching a certain age, will become senile, and lose most of their thinking and cognitive ability. That stereotype is simply not true. Most, in their later years, are actually more knowledgeable and are better thinkers than in their earlier years. They have gained experience and knowledge along the way, and can draw from that. They can use better judgement and plain common sense, mostly based on experience. You probably will, contrary to becoming senile, be able to speak, write and <u>think</u> with greater clarity and purpose.

> *"It is a man's fault, it is from want of use, if his mind grows torpid in old age."*
> — Samuel Johnson

> *"Iron rusts from disuse, stagnant water loses its purity and in cold weather becomes frozen even so does inaction sap the vigors of the mind."*
> — Leonardo Da Vinci

> *"Our minds can work for us or against us at any given moment. We can learn to accept and live with the natural psychological laws that govern us, understanding how to flow with life rather than struggle against it. We can return to our natural state of contentment."*
> — Richard Carlson

> *"The mind is like an iceberg, it floats with one-seventh of its bulk above water."*
> — Sigmund Freud

MEMORY: Memory is a product of the mind or brain, but we will consider it separately because loss of it is uppermost in many people's minds, and because there is a common fallacy or myth about it. The fallacy is that as you age, your memory fails in direct relation to your years, and could even be an indication you will have Alzheimer's. To start off with, I want you to ask yourself a question: "If my memory is indeed failing, how is it that I can recall past events, even back to childhood, with great clarity?"

There usually is some memory lapse as you age, but only to a degree — and that is generally self-inflicted. Memory lapse and memory loss are two entirely different things, and actual memory loss is generally insignificant in most individuals. Any effect on the memory is often due to other factors such as fatigue, stress, illness, simple memory overload, etc. Any memory lapse or loss does not indicate Alzheimer disease. Alzheimer is a disease, and memory impairment comes as a symptom or result of that disease.

Most memory lapses can be helped, if not eliminated by applying yourself to that section of the intellect dealing with memory, and exercising your memory ability. The old saying, "Use it or lose it," applies here, too. Memory problems are perhaps a sign of aging, but do not deserve the importance that many people place on them.

> *"Old men's eyes are like old men's memories; they are the strongest for things a long way off."*
> — George Eliot

> *"The best memory is that which forgets nothing, but injuries. Write kindness in marble and write injuries in the dust."*   — Persian Proverb

HEARING: Hearing loss is another distressing circumstance or problem. Note that I emphasized "loss" because nothing is lost until you are sure it's gone. The passage of years <u>might</u> bring a progressive loss of hearing to some, but it is not true that you are sure to have substantial hearing loss when you get to old age. It is true that our senses do become less acute with the passing years.

Some hearing loss is normal in the aging process, but a substantial loss or deafness is not a part of aging if proper care is taken. Much substantial loss or deafness is due to either damage from excessive noise in your occupation, damage from accidents, or not getting a progressive hearing problem rectified.

Deafness is terrible, and even partial deafness is distressing. It tends to make a person withdraw into a world of his/her own. This withdrawal can lead to other psychological problems.

If your hearing loss progresses to any degree that causes concern, have it checked thoroughly — by a specialist! The ear is a sensitive and delicate instrument — don't let anybody but a specialist poke around in it. Your problem might be nothing more than a simple build-up of wax, or it might be something serious, but fixable. Those are the only ears you are likely to get — take care of them.

First: If you have any sort of serious hearing loss at all — check it out! Preferably, go to a top-notch clinic such as the Shea Clinic (below). Their examination could very well come up with a solution to your problem. If they can't help you, they will tell you.

If your hearing cannot be corrected, then you should go to the next step — acquire and use a hearing aid. Too many at this point don't like an irritating hearing aid and simply don't use it. You must give it a fair amount of time to get used to it. All too many people have given up on hearing aids too soon before they master them, and lose some real assistance for their hearing problem.

Finally, if you refuse to use a hearing aid, you must learn to lip-read to the extent that your hearing is impaired. This is not an impossible task — many people have done so. The bottom line, don't give up on your hearing and withdraw into yourself. Any of the above steps will help you to stay in communication.

MY PERSONAL EXPERIENCE: I have always been blessed with excellent hearing ability, until these latter years. The only trouble I now have is "wax build-up." I have to have them cleaned out periodically, and am always surprised at the amount of wax the doctor digs out. (Incidentally, I get this done by a specialist also — they can remove the wax without pain or damage.)

My wife's (Geanie) hearing was a different matter. Her hearing in one ear kept getting progressively worse. Eventually, she had it checked by a specialist, who first found her basic problem. Finally, in 1998, we traveled to the Shea Clinic, in Memphis, Tennessee. She went through extensive examinations on the first day by Dr. Shea and his associates. That afternoon after the examinations, we met with Dr. Shea in his office. He said to my wife, "Geanie, you have 95% loss of hearing in one ear. The reason for this is that you have oto-sclerosis, a calcium buildup on the stapes—the little stirrup or "turning fork" of the ear. That's the bad news!" Then he grinned widely and said, "The good news is that we can fix it!", and went on to fully explain the operation in detail.

The next day, Dr. Shea performed a stapedectomy on Geanie. Later, when she felt well enough, we met with Dr. Shea again. He examined and tested her and proudly announced that she had recovered up to 95% of her hearing, and it would get better as she healed. He told us that her hearing was now better than the untreated one. It was great news.

I have told of this experience to encourage you to get hearing problems thoroughly checked out by specialists. I am sure there are other clinics as good, but I highly recommend Dr. Shea and the Shea Clinic in Memphis. I have been telling friends with hearing problems about this clinic. They will examine you and tell you honestly if they can help you. Dr. Shea is in his 70's, very active and brilliant, and loves what he is doing. He is the inventor of and holds over 50 patents on procedures for the ear, including the one used on Geanie. If you are interested in the cost factor, it was very reasonable — extremely and pleasantly so. It cost far less that this procedure and a two night stay in the hospital would cost.

TRAUMATIC PHASES OF LIFE

[When I refer to "traumatic phases," I am referring to two particular phases of life: middle age or "mid-life," and "retirement." The traumatic thing about mid-life is the well known mid-life crisis which some families go through. You wouldn't think retirement would be traumatic, but it is for many individuals. I will give my perceptions of both below.]

"MID-LIFE CRISIS": This is frustrating to write about or to suggest solutions, and it will be very short. What can you say to a person who is about to, or is making a complete fool out of him/herself to the point of complete humiliation of themselves and their family and close friends? There is probably nothing you can say that they will listen to. In this extreme self-gratification state, it is basically impossible to communicate with them. So, what advice can you give them?

Well, just in case one of "them" happen to be reading this, I am going to give the only sage and well thought out advice I can think of that will help. Here goes: "Snap out of it — get your head screwed on straight. You are on a path that you will regret for the rest of your life. It will possibly cost you your house, family, job, and everything else you strived for. Is it worth it? "

RETIREMENT: Some honestly look forward to retirement and some subconsciously dread it. At age of 65, there is no sudden decline in our abilities or strength. Others, generally younger, seem to think that is the case, however. The actual truth is that you are fine physically, still very capable, advanced mentally (and will advance more.) The real problems of retirement revolve around the mind set of those approaching and going into the retirement age.

Many look forward to retirement for the leisure time it affords. They may say, "Gosh, I can hardly wait. When I retire I am going to have lots of time for golfing, fishing, ...,etc." Some, when they reach that magical leisure point of retirement and plunge into those expected fulfilling pursuits—find that it isn't enough. You must find fulfillment, meaning, incentive and purpose — even in leisure.

Many have left their motivation in their once daily job or business and some incentives and goals must be substituted. Retirement should be a time of new opportunities and new goals. Often the question is "What can I do now for fulfilment?" Some will end up as couch-potatoes, drive their spouse crazy with their attitude and many times a long otherwise happy marriage ends in divorce.

There are, of course, many who have the right outlook and plans for their retirement and when they retire have an enjoyable time. They are rid of the pressures of earning a living and being a success, and have substituted activities, other incentives and purpose in their lives. This serves to keep their minds, body, and attitude healthy — thereby leading to an enjoyable life.

SOME POSITIVE SUGGESTIONS ABOUT RETIREMENT:

A. "ATTITUDE ADJUSTMENT": Have an "attitude adjustment!" If you have a negative outlook — turn it and adjust it to positive. You out-look toward life after retirement is crucial if you wish to have an enjoyable life.

B. DON'T RETIRE!: Yes, you heard me right, simply don't retire — change occupations! You probably don't need the extra income, but that is not the question. And don't let false pride get in the way of your enjoyment. You see many oldsters working at WalMart, etc., and they seem to be happy to be out among and meeting people. I would imagine many of these people had much more lucrative jobs and careers before they retired. You are doing this for yourself — for a more meaningful and enjoyable life.

C. GET INVOLVED!: Get involved in public, community and church programs or services to help others. For example: Pink Ladies at a hospital, "Meals on Wheels" for the disabled, visitation with the incapacitated in hospitals and retirement homes, to name just a few among the many things available. You will be surprised how fulfilling helping others will be.

D. DEVELOP YOUR TALENTS!: Many people have hidden or latent artistic or creative talents — develop yours! This could be in writing, painting, sculpting, leaded glass work, carving,--and many more creative talents. This could very well be a subconscious or latent desire of yours that can now be fulfilled.

Learn and do new manual creative crafts such as woodworking, plaster casting, metal work, etc. — it can be very time filling and self fulfilling.

If you don't already have a garden — start one! It is a great feeling to prepare, plant, nurture, and watch a garden grow.

E. BROADEN YOUR HORIZONS: Broaden your horizons and your mind by reading, perhaps something you had no time for before. There are more great books than you could possibly read in a lifetime. Also, get and learn to use a computer, and "surf" the Internet. This combined with reading will take you all over the world and enable you to see things you never dreamed of seeing before. Books and/or the Internet are like windows to the whole world.

> *"Growing old?-- Just a bad habit you wouldn't get if you kept busy."*

> *"The worst of work nowadays is what happens to people when they cease to work."*
> — Gilbert K. Chesterton

> *"A person can stand almost anything except a succession of ordinary days."*
> — Johann Wolfgang Von Goethe

> *"Sooner or later I'm going to die, but I'm not going to retire."*   — Margaret Mead

> *"Keep your enthusiasms, and forget your birthdays — that's the formula for staying young!"*

RELATIONSHIPS

> *"Happiness lies for those who cry, those who hurt, those who have searched, and those who have tried, for only they can appreciate the importance of people who have touched their lives."*

> *"Always put yourself in others' shoes. If you feel that it hurts you, it probably hurts the other person, too."*

Relationships are vital to your well-being regardless of age, but are especially valuable in your latter years. You must have friendship, love, and a feeling of connectedness — not only with your family, but with others as well. If you do not have family, then the other friendships become even more important. Let's discuss this relationship with family and others:

FAMILY FRIENDSHIP: Yes, you should be good friends with your family members. This may surprise some, but a healthy family relationship should be based on love as well as friendship. It is also important to be good friends with your spouse. You should enjoy sitting and visiting just as you would with a non-family friend. You are never too old to make your family your friends.

"Touching"is good in family relationships. Just a simple pat or touch says so much. It says, "I love you, and you are my good friend, too."

Hugging your spouse at least once a day is good. In fact, I recommend a one-minute non-sexual hug with your spouse a minimum of once a day. (*Non-sexual is the operative word here, and if you can hug for one minute without laughing you get extral points. You must try this!*) Hugs are also good with other family members. It is important for both male and female family to hug each other when meeting or before parting for a time.

FRIENDSHIP WITH OTHERS: You have no doubt heard the saying, "You can tell a man by his friends." That is very true. When you are older friends become even more dear and appreciated. Friends are especially important to those who have lost their spouses and/or other family members. They become that person's "support group."

Touching or hugging is good in non-family relationships, too. Just a simple pat or touch says so much. It says, "I love you as a friend," and/or "You are a good friend."

We need to realize how precious friendship really is, especially in our older years. A good friend is one who will listen and share your problems — getting them off your chest. For that matter, a good friend is one you can just sit with, not say anything, and feel like you have had good communication without verbalizing it. The bottom line is: Seek out and make friends — they really are more precious than gold.

> *[Our friendship "circle" is very dear and precious to me and my wife, especially so now that we are older. Mostly, they are the ones we met and formed bonds with at church. (This is the best place to meet, make friends, and build friendships.) Don't misunderstand, this group of friends is the "core," and it is not a closed group. We*

have many friends in our group that do not attend our church. We are always open to meeting and making new friends.

We love each other and thoroughly enjoy the company of any and all. We are "touchers" and "huggers," showing our affection for one another. We find many excuses to get together as a group: going to eat after church, going to McDonald's for snacks after evening Bible study, going on short trips together (even overnight.) I would say, other than the times mentioned, we get together, just to be together, an average of once every 3 weeks throughout the year.

We are a good support group, We share in one another's sad times (loss of loved ones, sickness, etc.), and in their good times (weddings, successes, etc.) (For instance, I had a recent book signing at a bookstore, and every one of those friends showed up and were happy for me. I was very grateful.)

We have had some who actually made the first overture to join our group, simply because they could see the genuine warmth, love and affection we have for each other. People are drawn to warmth. All in our group are open to others, because we believe that it is impossible to have too many friends.]

"An old man loved is winter with flowers."

"Those who love deeply never grow old; they may die of old age, but they die young."
—Benjamin Franklin

"Whenever you're in conflict with someone, there is one factor that can make the difference between damaging your relationship and deepening it. That factor is attitude."
—Timothy Bentley

IT'S ATTITUDE, ATTITUDE, ATTITUDE!

"Acceptance is the answer to all my problems today.

When I am disturbed, its because I find some person, place, thing, or situation—

Some fact of my life—unacceptable to me, and I can find no serenity until I accept that person, place, thing, or situation as being exactly the way it is supposed to be at this moment,

Nothing, absolutely nothing happens in God's world by mistake.

Unless I accept life completely on life's terms, I cannot be happy.

I need to concentrate not so much on what needs to be changed in the world as on what needs to be changed in me and in my attitudes."

—Author Unknown

"You are never too old to set another goal or to dream a new dream."

— Les Brown

God, when He created us "in His image," did so by making us rational, thinking, knowledgeable beings, unlike <u>any</u> other life (including apes) He created. In doing so, He gave us an extremely complex brain — the supreme organ of our bodies. The problem many have is ingesting drugs, alcohol, or other substances that affect the mind and take it out of our control — certainly not the intention of the Creator. Without harmful outside substances or activities, most can control their minds.

You can definitely control a stable mind in the matter of age. You are only as old as your mind. It has control of your body, and if the mind is old, the body will follow suit and be old. The body very definitely responds to the workings of the mind. So mind control is crucial, but certainly not impossible. One must choose to grow old gracefully if you wish to live your remaining life in happiness. Why would one choose otherwise and be sad, self-pitying, and even bitter as a way of life?

By the same token, your mind can remain young almost indefinitely. How does this happen? — by developing the right attitude. The attitude needed is one of humor, laughter, optimism, courage and perseverance. You must be both cheerful and realistic. Age will bring its progressive inherent problems — there is no doubt. Facing these problems with the correct attitude is the answer. Attitudes really control the conduct of our lives. They are a power that works at all times — for good or bad, so they must be controlled.

Bernard Baruch, in his eighties, was asked when one is old in age. His reply, "Old age is 15 years older than I am.", is evidence of this positive attitude. Remember the saying, "Be Happy." I firmly believe that when one door of happiness closes, another will always open. The problem comes with our attitude: — we spend so long looking at that closed door that we don't heed the one that is open for us. Look for the open doors of happiness. Let go of past failures and heartaches, and you will go on in life into a bright future.

If I asked you, "Would you like to spend what time you have left in life in a state of self pity, loneliness, bitterness and abject misery?" — what would your answer be? I would hope that your answer would be, "Absolutely not!" Of course you would not, if sane, opt for a life of misery. The way to negate such a life is the right positive attitude. Actually the most important decision you can make at this phase in your life is your choice of attitude.

Live your life with the right attitude toward it, and I promise you— when you die you will be smiling, and many who are left will be crying because of your demise.

> *"I am not afraid of tomorrow, for I have seen yesterday and I love today."*
>   — William Allen White

"Expect the best! It lies not in the past.
 God ever keeps the good wine till the last.
Beyond are nobler work and sweeter rest.
 Expect the best!"
                                    —William Pierson Merrill

"When you see an old man amiable, mild, equable, con-
tent, and good-humored, be sure that in his youth he has
been just, generous, and forbearing. In his end he does
not lament the past, nor dread the future; he is like the
evening of a fine day."

Let's look as some the facets, results and evidences of the positive attitude:

"HEALTHY" ATTITUDE

Many worry too much about their health. It is a sad state when one wor-
ries so much about their health that they can't enjoy life. In fact, since
mind has so much control over the body, too many people worry themselves into more serious health problems.

I have Osteoarthritis and Rheumatoid Arthritis. The regular arthritis
(Osteoarthritis) is a minor irritation compared to the RA (Rheumatoid.)
They do not know what triggers RA and they have no cure for it, only
medication to keep it under control.

I feel that I have a healthy attitude toward my problems. I base it
on that old adage: "I used to be sorry for myself because I had no shoes
— until I met a man who had no feet!" I am very thankful for the good
health I have because I don't have to look very far to see someone with
much greater health problems than I. You will not catch me trying to
draw sympathy by saying I feel bad, because most of the time I feel
good — considering. I have always felt that laying a trip on others will
not make me feel one iota better, and I am afraid I might get to believing my ills are worse than they are if I expound on them. The bottom
line: I am content with what I have been dealt and feel lucky to receive
that and no more.

"Our attitudes control our lives. Attitudes are a secret power working twenty-four hours day, for good or bad. It is of paramount importance that we know how to harness and control this great force."

— Tom Blandi

"There is little difference in people, but that little difference makes a big difference. That little difference is attitude. The big difference is whether it is positive or negative. "

— W. Clement Stone

HUMOR & LAUGHTER

"Laugh a little now and then
It brightens life a lot;
You can see the brighter side
Just as well as not.

Don't go mournfully around,
Gloomy and forlorn;
Try to make your fellow men
Glad that you were born."

"The happiest of people don't necessarily have the best of everything; they just make the most of everything that comes along their way."

"I am persuaded that every time a man smiles— but much more so when he laughs— it adds something to this fragment of life."

— Laurence Sterne

"Laughter is the tonic, the relief, the surcease for pain."
— Charlie Chaplin

HUMOR is one of the important facets that go to make a positive outlook. It really is a must that you enjoy what life you have left, by not dwelling on the past, nor fearing the future, but by seeing humor in the present — even in perhaps embarrassing circumstances, yours and others. A sense of humor and the ability and readiness to laugh at yourself is a valuable asset in handling some of the unpleasant circumstances that come along the aging journey. Enjoyment of life even when you have reached old age is possible, in spite of your present circumstances.

LAUGHTER has been proved to be good for your health — physical and mental. Physically, it increases breathing, and thereby the supply of oxygen — having an effect somewhat like fast walking. It has been said that it is "like jogging on the inside."

Laughter is good for mental health. It's really hard to dwell on your own problems and troubles when you are laughing. It has been said that "if you don't laugh at problems, you will have nothing to laugh at when you get to an older age." Laughter has been proven to be a tonic for your mind and will relieve tensions.

Laughter is hard to do alone. Others are needed to watch, hear or react in order to make it worthwhile. Others are drawn to and like to be near someone who laughs and perhaps makes them laugh. It tends to be therapeutic for all concerned. It definitely eases painful burdens. I sincerely believe that God gave us laughter to relieve the tensions and pressures of life, and to add sparkle and zest to our lives.

> *"Seek out every opportunity for laughter that you can, for laughter is one of those things, like music and flowers, that God has given us to relieve the tensions that we undergo in this life."*
> — Preston Bradley

> *"People who laugh actually live longer than those who don't laugh. Few persons realize that health actually varies according to the amount of laughter."*
> —Dr. James Walsh

> *"I can't imagine a wise old person who can't laugh."*
> — Erik H Erikson

LIFE & LIVING

"Fear less, hope more; eat less, chew more; whine less, breathe more; hate less, love more; and all good things are yours."   *— Swedish Proverb*

"When the door of happiness closes, another opens, but often times we look so long at the closed door that we don't see the one which has been opened for us."

"The happiest of people don't necessarily have the best of everything; they just make the most of everything that comes along their way."

The way you look at or respond to every day events is an important facet of life. Do you fully realize what the sage meant when he said, "Stop and smell the roses?' To live life as it should be lived you must equate it with a fine wine.

I am not a wine drinker, but my understanding is that to fully enjoy aged wine, it must be imbibed in a certain way. First you must let your smelling sense appreciate the "bouquet" of this fine wine, before it even touches your lips. Then, you very slowly sip it, savoring both the bouquet and taste. If you gulp it down, it might as well be cheap beer.

That is the essence of getting the most out of life. Life is to be savored and sipped — not gulped down. True happiness in life is not to be found in go, go, go to various functions and events—spending all your time seeking something that is actually around you already. True happiness is found in small "sips," the small things you can do all day, every day—read a good book, go on a picnic in the park, take a walk and enjoy God's creation, enjoy a quiet meal and talk with your spouse or other family members, meet and visit friends, etc. These are just a few of the many small things or "sips" you can enjoy. True, deep happiness can be found in the small things of life.

Another crucial factor in living and savoring life is simply to be content. Don't stew and fret and strive for more than you really need. Whatever you have — be <u>content</u> with it. Contrary to popular opinion, wealth and possessions do not inherently bring happiness. It is not to say that you can't have happiness if you have wealth and possessions — it's how you view what you have. If you are content with what you have, you will be happy. If more possessions are your driving incentive you will not find true happiness, because you will not be content with what you have.

Let's look at Howard Hughes. At one time, he was perhaps the wealthiest man in the world. He was always wanting to amass more, and was always fearful that others were trying to take some of his wealth. He ended up later in his life with more inhibitions, complexes, dreads of disease and poisoning that it first ruined his mind. He ended up, long before his death, a more pitiful human creature than you could find living on the streets of any city. Do I envy the man with all that wealth? — No, I merely pity him. My mind, body, and the savoring of life and living is just too precious and too high a price to pay. I would rather be content with what I have. I have seen many very happy people who don't necessarily have the best of things, but they do make the most of what they have.

You have only one life to live. Handle it with care and use it wisely: With your ability and resources, do what you want to do, be what you want to be and go where you want to go. It's up to you and your sense of values. You can work long hours, strive, worry and get stressed out, and you will probably end up with a large bank account. Perhaps you will be lucky and have enough funds to pay for the high priced medical and other care you may require for abusing your physical body and mind. You might even get real lucky and be able to pay for your care in a retirement home. Want to take the gamble?

> *"May you have enough happiness to make you sweet,*
> *enough trials to make you strong, enough sorrow to*
> *keep you human, enough hope to make you happy."*

"Let us see to it .... that our lives, like jewels of great price, be noteworthy not because of their width, but because of their weight. Let us measure them by their performance, not their duration."
— Seneca

"This is the precept by which I have lived: Prepare for the worst; expect the best; and take what comes."
—Robert E. Speer

"The brightest future will always be based on a forgotten past, you can't go on well in life until you let go of your past failures and heartaches."

OPTIMISM

"An optimist laughs to forget; the pessimist forgets to laugh."

Too many people deal too much with the negative — with what is wrong with their lives. I am a believing and practicing optimist, and highly recommend it. Why not try to see positive things, — things that will empower and motivate you to live the life of your dreams. Set goals and expect to reach them, and become the person you want to be. Optimism is the driving force.

"Nothing in life is so hard that you can't make it easier by the way you take it."
— Ellen Glasgow

"Between the optimist and the pessimist, the difference is droll.
The optimist sees the doughnut; the pessimist the hole!"
— Mclandburgh Wilson

"Optimism is the cheerful frame of mind that enables a teakettle to sing, though in hot water up to its nose."
"An optimist may see a light where there is none, but why must the pessimist always run to blow it out?"
— Michel De Saint-Pierre

TIME

"As the bird trims to the gale,
I trim myself to the storm of time,
I man the rudder, reef the sail,
Obey the voice at eve obeyed at prime"
"Lowly faithful, banish fear,
Right onward drive unharmed;
The port, well worth the cruise, is near,
And every wave is charmed."
— *Ralph Waldo Emerson*

"Time — our youth — it never really goes, does it? It is all held in our minds."
— *Helen Santmyer*

Time is an integral part of life and living, and how you use it (or abuse it) is critical. Many people are very judicious in how they spend money, but very careless in how they spend their time. Time is much more precious than money. You can recoup any loss in money — but not time. Once time is spent, it is gone forever. You often hear people refer to "saving time." Did you ever stop to think and realize that saving time is actually impossible. You can make the most of it, savor it, and fill it with joy and enjoyment — but you can't save it.

Time is a precious possession. There is no doubt that we all have a certain amount of time allotted to us in this life. Some may have a lot of time left, but many others have very little. The disturbing thing is that one does not know when his allotment of time is running out. That is why we should be extremely prudent in how we spend it — because we often waste it.

Do you have any regrets for not having spent more quality time with your children, your spouse, your friends, or just "smelling the roses?" You should use that as a lesson and change your outlook on time. Treat it like fine wine: very carefully pour (allot or spend) it, savor it to the fullest, and make the utmost of it.

Take Time

Take time to live; it is one secret of success.
Take time to think; it is the source of power.
Take time to play; it is the secret of youth.
Take time to read; it is the foundation of knowledge.
Take time for friendship; it is a source of happiness.
Take time to laugh; it helps lift life's load.
Take time to dream; it hitches the soul to the stars.
Take time to worship; it is the highway to reverence.
Take time to pray; it helps bring God near and washes
the dust of earth from our eyes.

"You can't turn back the clock, but you can wind it up again."

If I Had My Life To Live Over Again ...

I would have talked less and listened more.
I would have invited friends over to dinner even if
the carpet was stained and the sofa faded.
I would have eaten the popcorn in the 'good' living
room and worried much less about the dirt when
someone wanted to light a fire in the fireplace.
I would have taken the time to listen to my grandfather
ramble about his youth.
I would never have insisted the car windows
be rolled up on a summer day because my
hair had just been teased and sprayed.
I would have burned the pink candle sculpted
like a rose before it melted in storage

I would have sat on the lawn with my children
and not worried about grass stains.
I would have cried and laughed less while watching
television and more while watching life.
I would have shared more of the responsibility
carried by my husband.
I would have gone to bed when I was sick instead
of pretending the earth would go into a holding
pattern if I weren't there for the day.
I would have never bought anything just because
it was practical, wouldn't show soil or was
guaranteed to last a lifetime.
Instead of wishing away nine months of pregnancy,
I'd have cherished every moment and realized
that the wonderment growing inside me was
the only chance in life to assist God in a miracle.
When my kids kissed me impetuously, I would never
have said, "Later ... Now go get washed up for
dinner."
There would have been more "I love you's" more
"I'm sorry's" but mostly, given another shot at
life, I would seize every minute ... look at it and
really see it and live it ... and never give it
back.

— Erma Bombeck

DEATH and SPIRITUALITY

[I am closing this book by openly discussing our "last
performance" in this life as we know it. This final act is,
of course, our own inevitable death — something that is
on the mind of every adult to a degree, and to a progres-
sively higher degree as we age. One should be aware of
the final act of death in their aging process — in this life.

To me, as a Christian, this is not a finality. The follow-
ing discussion is my personal testimony. I believe in eter-

nal life and being prepared for life after death, and I am going to discuss it in a very personal way. If my words offend anybody, I do not apologize—I have to write what I believe and what I know, in my mind, will help those facing the inevitability of their own death.]

"When you were born, you were crying and everyone around you was smiling. Live your life so that when you die, you're the one who is smiling and everyone around you is crying."

When you are young, you feel invincible and the awareness or thought of your own death is way back in your mind — hardly ever thought of. This is in spite of the evidence we see every day of people of all ages being killed by accident, or dying from some disease. The closer you get to old age, the more aware you are of your own impending demise.

All adults fear death to a lesser or higher degree. I believe they not so much fear the very act of dying as they do the unknown of the before and after. They worry about and fear the before because they do not know how they will die. Will it be painful? — a long-lasting illness? — sudden? These are all unknowns, and people quite naturally have some fear of the unknown.

Many fear what happens after death. As Christians, we have nothing to fear. We have the assurance that we are in Eternity right now and death is just a passage to be with the Lord, and there will no longer be any pain, stress or worry. That is our simple belief, thus we don't fear death as being the end of everything.

When you think about your own death, which I often do, there are some important questions to ask yourself — and act on them if needed. They are:

    A. Do I have a healthy spirituality? — a right relationship or walk with God?

    B. Are there broken or damaged relationships I need to repair or reconcile: family, friends, associates, co-workers?

    C. Are there words I need to speak, or actions or gestures I need to use, to show someone that I love them?

    D. Do I need to make amends for something or reconcile for an offense with any person?

I believe that we should ask ourselves these questions and act on all of them if necessary, in order to face our own inescapable death with a serene and positive attitude.

You can develop a good attitude toward death—a positive one bolstered by the assurance of a life hereafter if you are a Christian. If you aren't a Christian, I pray you would investigate that possibility. It really is a very simple decision to make and a simple action to take.

A PRAYER, WRITTEN BY A NUN

Lord, Thou knowest better than I myself know that I am
*   growing older and will some day be old.*
Keep me from the fatal habit of thinking I must say
*   something on every subject an on every occasion.*
Release me from the craving to straighten out every-
*   body's affairs.*
Make me thoughtful, but not moody; helpful, but not
*   bossy.*
With my vast store of wisdom it seems a pity not to use
*   it all, but Thou knowest, O Lord, that I want a few*
*   friends at the end.*
Keep my mind free from the recital of endless details;
*   give me wings to get to the point.*
Seal my lips on my aches and pains. They are increas-
*   ing, and love of rehearsing them is becoming sweet-*
*   er as the days go by.*
I dare not as fro grace enough to enjoy the tales of oth-
*   ers' pains, but help me to endure them with*
*   patience.*
I do not ask for an improved memory, but for a growing
*   humility and a lessening cocksureness when my*
*   memory seems to clash with the memories of others.*
Teach me the glorious lesson that occasionally I may
*   be mistaken.*
Keep me reasonably sweet; I do not want to be a saint
*   — some of them are so hard to live with — but a*
*   sour old person is one of the crowning works of the*
*   devil.*
Give me the ability to see good things in unexpected
*   places, and talents in unexpected people.*
And give me, O Lord, the grace to tell them so.

Amen

"As for old age, embrace and love it. It abounds with pleasure if you know how to use it. The gradually declining years are among the sweetest in a man's life; and I maintain that even when they have reached the extreme limit, they have their pleasure still."
                                        — Seneca

[Well, I have presented my "case" for the process of aging. I have tried to present it, as best I can, from both a humorous and positive perspective, because that's how one facing aging should look at it. I have also tried to present it with a realistic but optimistic approach, because we all should approach it from that angle.

My motive in writing this book is to perhaps instill in others the positive and optimistic way I feel about aging. I am truly enjoying my golden years with my wife, Geanie (married 53 years.) In fact, my love for her has grown deeper. I am enjoying these years in spite of some medical problems — which I think go with the territory. I want to help others to enjoy their golden years in the same way.

I will be happy to continue to help and thus am opening myself up to questions, comments, etc. I am putting my name, address and e-mail address below. If you write, I will answer as soon as possible. If you e-mail — I will answer that also. I will personally talk to you should our paths cross.

Keep this in mind: I am not a professional doctor, psychologist, counselor, or anything else — except perhaps a "professional aged person." Any advice I give regarding those areas could be worth what you paid for it — nothing. Any advice I give on being or becoming a

*Christian, you can "put in the bank," because you
don't have to be a professional on that to advise.*

*Thank you for buying my book, and may God Bless and
Keep you.]*

Les Blair
709 Airport Rd.
Osage Beach, MO 65065
E-mail: pflats@lakeozark.net

BOOKS BY LES BLAIR

"Ma' Cookin'"
Lots of good recipes, spiced with old time cures, sayings and superstitions. Very popular. Over 1 3/4 million copies sold and still selling.
Copyright 1966 — 56 pages.   Price: $3.75 (postpaid) each

"Mom's Cookin'"
Filled with unusual and delicious country recipes, shared by some mighty good cooks, and spiced with country sayings.
Copyright 1986 — 64 pages   Price: $3.75 (postpaid) each

"Mom's Best"
Brim full of more good country cooking and spiced with more country sayings. No duplication of recipes or sayings.
Copyright 1986 — 64 pages   Price: $3.75 (postpaid) each

"Jest Tawk"
A book you will thoroughly enjoy, one that gives the pronunciation and usage of old time country words. Spiced with old time, down to earth, country sayings.
Copyright 1986 — 52 pages   Price: $3.75 (postpaid) each

"Talkin' Dirty"
You will enjoy this book from cover to cover. It does not have vulgarity, but it is filled with very graphic and colorful phrases and expressions used by rural folks. These very vivid and picturesque phrases have been remembered and collected over man years.
Copyright 1989 — 64 pages   Price: $3.75 (postpaid) each

"Beyond Thyme: Herbs, Spices and "Stuff"
You can really put "some spice in your life" by the addition of herbs and spices to your cooking. This book removes the mystery of the use of herbs and spices.
Copyright 1992 — 72 pages   Price: $3.75 (postpaid) each

"Gettysburg . . . the beginning of the end."
This well-written narrative of the great battle of Gettysburg is easy to read and captures the reader's attention quickly. It lists the sequence of events in this great historical battle and reveals the colorful personalities of many of the military Generals. The text is enhanced with maps and pictures.
Copyright 1995 — 88 pages   Price: $6.00 (postpaid) each

"South of the Border" — Tex-Mex Cookin'"
A compilation of recipes from Texas and Mexico. Many of the recipes have been adapted to the popular Tex-Mex cooking. You'll wanthis cookbook for your library. The recipes are clearly written and easy to prepare.
Copyright 1995 — 72 pages   Price: $3.75 (postpaid) each

"Ha Ha Tonka — Land of the Laughing Water"
An exciting historical account of the land and inhabitants of Ha Ha Tonka. Fictional characters combined with actual events narrate many enjoyable stories about actual events which took place in the region now known as the Ozarks in Missouri.
Copyright 2000 — 150 pages   Price: $13.00 (postpaid) each

"Peace 'n' Plenty" — by Roxie Kelly & Les Blair
This great cookbook was orginally compiled by Roxie Kelly, an excellant cook. Les Blair acquired all rights to this book and completely revised and improved it. Many excellent recipes have been added and sayings have been added for interest.
Copyright 2003 — 152 pages   Price: $10.95 (postpaid) each

"Old As Dirt — So What!"
Les Blair is convinced that one needs to be equipped with three things to face the aging clock and its problems,--a healthy spirituality, a positive attitude and a quick sense of humor. He has approached old age with a wonderful "tongue in cheek" humor in the first parts of this book, but also seriously looks at a better way to approach the inevitable aging process.
Copyright 2003 — 128 pages   Price: $10.95 (postpaid) each

LES BLAIR PUBLICATIONS — **Les & Geanie Blair**
709 Airport Road — **Osage Beach, MO 65065**
Ph.: (573) 348-3677 — **E-Mail: pflats@lakeozark.net**
Web-site: www.lesblair.com